The book "Latvia, the Land We Love" in English.
The book was compiled and published by *Nacionālais Apgāds* Ltd.
Maija Šetlere managed the project.
Artist: Alda Zunde
Photographer: Andris Eglītis
Texts by Anna Šmite
Computers: Mārtiņš Zunde, Vanda Voiciša
Computer operator: Daina Freimantāle
English translation: Henrijs Rūsis
English language editor: Viesturs Pauls Karnups
Director: Dagnija Vanaga

The book was published under the editorship
of Pēteris Apinis and Maija Šetlere.

Photographs by Aigars Altenbergs, Pēteris Apinis, Leons Balodis, Māra
Brašmane, Lauris Filics, Mihails Gleizers, Gvido Kajons, Juris Kalniņš, Dainis
Kārkluvalks, Valts Kleins, Raimo Lielbriedis, Aivars Liepiņš, Alberts Linarts,
Ainars Meiers, Uldis Pāže, Artūrs Pērkons, Imants Prēdelis, Rihards Puriņš,
Romvalds Salcevičs, Valdis Semjonovs, Indriķis Stūrmanis, Anita Tukiša,
Jānis Vītiņš, Ilmārs Znotiņš and Vilnis Zilberts were used in the book.

The book was printed by the *Jāņa sēta* printing house of the stock company
Preses nams in *Cēsis*.

ISBN 9984-26-040-2

Latvia
the land we love

Latvia is a 64 589 square km large country on the eastern coast of the Baltic Sea. The independent Latvian State was proclaimed on 18 November 1918, for the first time. The army of the USSR entered Latvia on 17 June 1940, and it was occupied and annexed. Latvia was occupied by the Nazi Germany during World War II and again by the Soviet army in 1945. The Latvian Supreme Council adopted Declaration of Independence on 4 May 1990, and independence was renewed on 21 August 1991 after the failure of the Russian coup d'ttat and the collapse of the Soviet Union. The Constitution (*Satversme*) of Latvian State was reinstated in 1993.

The parliament – *Saeima* – is the supreme legislative power of the country. Vaira Vīķe-Feiberga is the President of Latvia since 1999. In the upper part of the shield of Latvia's coat of arms there is a sun symbol, while the bottom part is divided into two areas – the first contains a red lion on a silver background, while the second shows a silver griffin on a red background. The flag of Latvia is dark red with a narrow white horizontal band through the middle. The colour proportions are 2:1:2. The first occasion the flag was used was in 1279, described in the *Livonian Rhymed Chronicle*. The use of the flag was banned during the Soviet occupation and people were deported to Siberia for keeping one. The Latvian National Anthem was written during the national awakening of the Latvian people in the 19th century. The words and music were written by Kārlis Baumanis.

Rīga is the capital of Latvia, populated by about one million people. It is located at the place where the *Daugava* River flows into the Gulf of Rīga. Latvian culture is based around Latvian folklore, which is influenced by West European, North European and Slavic cultures. Latvian folklore's greatest treasure is the 1.4 million folksongs – *Dainas*, gathered and compiled by Krišjānis Barons in late-19th century.

Latvian is the official language in the Republic of Latvia. It is an ancient Indo-European language, which belongs to the Baltic group of languages. Latvia is traditionally divided into four regions – Vidzeme, Kurzeme, Latgale and Zemgale with *Sēlija*. There are 26 district and more than 600 town and parish local governments in Latvia. The seven largest cities – Rīga, *Daugavpils*, *Liepāja*, *Ventspils*, *Jelgava*, *Rēzekne* and *Jūrmala* – fulfil the functions of both district and city local governments in their territories.

The combined length of the national borders is 1865 km. The length of land borders is 1370 km: the Northern border with Estonia – 337 km, the Eastern with Russia – 292 km, the South-eastern with Belarus – 171 km, and the Southern with Lithuania – 570 km. The length of sea borders is 495 km. The maximum length of Latvia's territory in a West – East direction is 450 km, in a North – South direction – 210 km.

The distance on an imaginary straight line from Rīga to Vilnius is 267 km, to Tallinn – 280 km, to Helsinki – 365 km, to Stockholm – 445 km, to St. Petersburg – 490 km, to Warsaw – 540 km, to Berlin – 840 km, to Moscow – 850 km, to Oslo – 860 km, to London – 1660 km.

The highest point above sea level in Latvia is *Gaiziņš* Hill – 311.5 m. The average yearly temperature in Latvia is 5.6°C. The highest temperature was recorded in *Jelgava*, 1994 – plus 36°C, the lowest – in *Zosēni*, 1979 – minus 42.9°C. The average level of annual rainfall is 657 mm. The thickest cover of snow was recorded in *Stende* – 87 cm.

The *Daugava* River is the largest river in Latvia. It is 1020 km long and flows through Russia, Belarus and 357 km though the territory of Latvia. The *Gauja* River is 452 km long and runs only through Latvia. A 20-km long section of the river serves as a natural border between Latvia and Estonia. Lake *Lubāns* is Latvia's largest in terms of area covered, while Lake *Rāzna* is the richest in water – 405 million square m. Lake *Drīdzis* is the deepest one – 65.1 m.

The lats is the national currency in Latvia. It is the world's strongest currency, attached to the IMF's international currency basket and SDR, and fully secured by gold and foreign currency reserves. One Trojan ounce of gold costs 162.72 lats. 100 lats are equal to 125.05 units of SDR. Considering the average currency rate fluctuations, 100 lats are worth 106 British pounds, 170 Euro, USD 172, DM 323, 1456 SEK, 4800 Russian roubles.

The Order of the Three Stars (*Triju Zvaigžņu ordenis*) is the highest form of Latvia's National Honours.

Information about Latvia is available on the Internet – www.latvia.lv, but the most detailed information is presented in the book *Latvia. Country. Nation. State* by Pēteris Apinis. Information about the book may be requested at www.nma.lv

The Rīga Castle

The Rīga castle houses representation premises for the president of Latvia Vaira Vīķe-Freiberga

Few lands have experienced tougher challenges during the last few centuries than Latvia. Few monuments to history testify of the fate of a land and people more truthfully than does the Rīga castle. The foundation to the castle was laid in 1330. A triplex fortified building with an inner yard and four towers housed an alien power, determined to subjugate the local people. The master of the Livonian Order lived here until 1429 and later as well. The citizens destroyed the castle in the 15th century. It was rebuilt only in 1515. Sculptural reliefs, resembling the Order's patroness St. Maria and the Order's master V. Platenberg, are remarkable monuments to medieval sculpture.

The Rīga castle was rebuilt many times during the next centuries. Large-scale construction works were carried out during the Swedish period, especially between 1625 and 1682, as well as during the subsequent Russian period. In 1818, the front part of the castle was re-fitted as representation premises for the governor-general of Vidzeme. The castle lost the functions of a separate fortified entity with the fall of Livonian Order. It became part of the fortification system of the city. The fortification moats were filled over in the 18th century and the castle square was built during the end of the century. Polish, Swedish and Russian governor-generals lived in the castle from 1562 until 1917.

The rooms in the Rīga castle were fitted out by architect E. Laube to suit the representation needs of the government during the first independent Latvian state (1938). The castle became the official home of the President of Latvia. The Lead Tower, White Room and Red Room were partly restored during the years of Soviet occupation. Several museums and the Pioneers castle shared space here.

Now the Rīga castle again serves the representation needs of the President of Latvia, as well as being home to several museums.

The Freedom Monument

The Freedom Monument stands in the centre of Rīga. It was built with voluntary donations during the first period of the independent Latvian state (1918 – 1940) and became a symbol of Latvian people's love of the fatherland and an expression of the longing for freedom. On the way towards a renewed, independent Latvia the people gained strength and unity at gatherings by the Freedom Monument. The Freedom Monument witnessed both the tragedies and the moments of glory of the nation, such as the declaration of the renewal of statehood on the 4 May 1990 and the declaration of independence on 21 August 1991. The Freedom Monument with its international fame has the power to inspire everyone, but to a Latvian, it is a place that expresses the sacred spiritual strength of the nation and a place where to gather on occasions important to the Latvian State. The placing of flowers at the base of the monument has become a tradition for graduates, brides and grooms – it is a sacred place, where for a Latvian *te akmens runu runā* ("here the stone is speaking"). *Akmens ... Dievu lūdz ...* ("the stone ... prays to God ...")

A dedication to Fatherland and Freedom is engraved on the main plate of the monument. The monument is 42.7 m high (by sculptor Kārlis Zāle and architect Ernests Štālbergs, 1931 – 1935). The classic obelisk is a significant work of art by Zāle, expressing the values of the Latvian people and their belief in the future of the nation. The composition of the monument consists of sculptural groups on several levels. The sculptures reveal symbols of nation's longing for freedom and the hundreds of years of struggles against oppressors. National visions, heroes (*Lāčplēsis* ("Bearslayer"), *Važu rāvējs* ("the Chainbreaker"), *Latvija, Vaidelotis* ("the kokle player") and historic events (the year 1905 ("First Russian revolution"), the battle against *bermontiešiem* ("the soldiers of General Bermonts –1919") on *Dzelzstilts* ("Iron") bridge) are symbolically displayed in sculptures and reliefs. The 19-m obelisk is topped with the 9-m figure of Freedom with three upheld gold stars. The stars symbolise the three main Latvian regions – Kurzeme, Vidzeme, and Latgale. Sophisticated dynamics of expression and characters is achieved by utilising polychromatic techniques. The figure of Freedom can be seen from many angles, even as a reflection in the waters of the city canal.

Rīga – the Capital of Latvia, a City with 800 Years of History

Rīga is the capital of the Republic of Latvian, located on the left bank of the *Daugava* River where it flows into the Gulf of Rīga. One of the distinctive hallmarks of Rīga is its skyline silhouette – three high spires raising above the line of the banks of the *Daugava* – the church towers of the Dom Cathedral, St. Peter's and St. Jacob's. The concluding element on the left of the skyline is the Rīga castle of the Order of the Brotherhood of the Sword (1330). These days the church towers are higher than they used to be. The ones of the Grieving Maria's, St. Maria Magdalene's, Anglican, St. John's and the Reformers' Churches and the building of Rīga's Technical University are in the central part of the skyline. The skyline of Old Rīga which is characteristic of Rīga, is a value to be preserved. In 1997, it was included in UNESCO's World cultural heritage list.

Livs and Kurs lived here 2000 years ago. The German merchants who arrived in late 12th century found the peninsula formed by the Rīga river flowing into the *Daugava* River suitable for settlement. The Chronicle of Indrikis mentions the site of Rīga for the first time as the battlefield where Liv chieftain Imanta (Imauts) slew German bishop Berthold in 1198. His successor bishop Albert chose Rīga as the new centre of his bishopric in 1201. This year is seen as the year of Rīga's foundation. German merchants and craftsmen settled here. St. Peter's Church was first mentioned in 1209, the foundations of the Dom Cathedral were laid in 1211 outside of the German settlements, St. Jacob's Church was built in 1225. Trade was the source of the prosperity of the city. Rīga played a major part in the Hanseatic League during the 14th century. The rulers changed in Latvia and so did the ones in Rīga – Germans, Danes, Poles, Swedes, and Russians. During the many centuries, Rīga has become one of the most beautiful cities of Europe, often called *Little Paris*. Old Rīga, the parks along the canal, the boulevards around the old city (a project by architects Johan Daniel Felsco and Otto Diche from 1856), the wooden architecture in *Pārdaugava*, *Mežparks*, art nouveau buildings and many parks and gardens make Rīga unique and interesting. The number of inhabitants has changed a great deal during centuries. Between the 13th and the 18th century the inhabitants were mostly Germans and Latvians. Only at the end of the 19th and the beginning of the 20th century, were Latvians the dominant group in the city. Rīga is now a multicultural city with about 800 000 inhabitants.

An ancient legend tells that every year a dwarf comes out of the *Daugava* River and asks the people: *Is Rīga finished yet?* The answer has to be: *No, it is not.* If anyone should ever say it is, Rīga would sink into the *Daugava* River with all its buildings and stones.

Song Festivals Bring Tens of Thousands of Singers and Hundreds of Thousands of Listners from All Over Latvia Together on the Great Arena Every Five Years

Latvians are a singing nation - song accompanies them both in work and on holidays. Song is a way to express joy and happiness, when sad it helps to put the blues away, it gives strength and unity to the nation during important turning points in history.

The song festival movement in Latvia was started by united choirs in *Dikļi*, 1864, followed by the First Song Festival of Kurzeme in *Dobele*, 1870. The repertoire was chiefly composed of church songs.

The First General Song Festival of Latvia took place in Rīga, 1873. The festival was organised by Rīga Latvian Society. Some 45 choirs and the *Irlava* teachers' seminar orchestra, conducted by Jānis Bētiņš, all took part. There were song wars as well. The repertoire included church songs, Latvian folksongs adapted by Jānis Cimze, original songs by Kārlis Baumais, songs Franz Schubert and other non-Latvian composers. Indriķis Zīle and Jānis Bētiņš were the leading conductors. The festival was the beginning of a lasting tradition — of the gathering from all parts of Latvia to express the creative spirit of the people and belief in the future of a unified nation. The tradition of song festivals was not broken by the Soviet authorities, although the idea of the festival was ruthlessly manipulated with. The ten festivals during this period were a form of protest against the authorities and against spiritual oppression. Latvians were free to express themselves only through song. The XX Song Festival of 1990 was held at the peak of the third *Atmoda* (Awakening) movement and the transition to independence, while the XXI and XXII festivals (1993, 1998) were celebrated once more in an independent state.

Latvian folk costumes are seen as various and colourful as ever during the days of song and folk dance festivals. Latvian farmers lived tied to the land in a specific region in the 17th to 19th centuries. All the necessary items were made using local resources. These conditions gave rise to ethnographic diversity with different methods of work, clothing design, ornaments, and choice in colours affected by the natural environment. Every region has distinct and different folk costumes.

Folk Dance Festival

Latvian folk dances are an ancient and lively form of cultural tradition. In 1937, the Latvian Home Guard organised the first folk dance and gymnastics festival in Rīga, which was attended by 20 folk dance groups with 720 dancers. The first dancing competitions took place.

Folk Dance Festivals were staged along with Song Festivals after World War II. Despite the part of the repertoire enforced by an alien ideology, the festival was always accompanied with certain elements of national self-assertion and protest. In 1948, a major folk dance performance was staged as a part of the 11th Song Festival, and this performance was seen as the first national folk dance festival. These festivals are theatrical, and they have become a traditional way of demonstrating Latvian folk dances. There have been 11 folk dance festivals so far, and smaller events are held in Latvia's districts and regions. Festivals are held for the various generations, including the elderly and schoolchildren, and there are special events for trade school students and university students.

The festivals are always enjoyable for the easy and quick dance step, excellent choreography and the splendid folk costumes. The total number of dancers at a folk dance festival is about 10 000. The dancers come together in groups for the young, middle and older generations. Usually there are two repertoires, one for regional folk dances and the other one for experimental, creative dances, where folklore and ethnographic material is the starting point for excellent contemporary choreographic works.

Folk dance groups are active in all parts of Latvia. They become particularly active as the next Song and Folk Dance festival approaches, but folk dance performances are a regular part at various public events, concerts, and competitions in Latvia and abroad. Today there are some 825 folk dance groups with some 20 000 participants in Latvia.

Much credit for improving folk dance traditions goes to the choreographers: Ingrīda Saulīte, Imants Magone, Uldis Šteins and Uldis Žagata.

Rīga is one of the greenest European cities. The park architects George Kufalt and Andrejs Zeidaks were founders of European continental park culture. Rīga's fortification walls were torn down in 1857, and all the debris was piled up to make a hill by the canal, which is now known as *Bastejkalns*. The channel parks around *Vecrīga* have become the symbol of the green Rīga. All of Rīga's parks are complete works of art with tidy lawns, massive flowerbeds with winter-hardy plants and selected varieties of trees and bushes.

Bastejkalns

Bastejkalns or *Gliemežnicas kalns* (Cockleshell Hill), as it was called in the beginning because of its spiralled walkways is an artificial elevation in the park zone between Riga city channel and *Basteja bulvāris*. *Bastejkalns* was created at the site previously known as *Smilšu bastions* (Sand Bulwark) from debris left behind after Riga's fortification walls were torn down in the 19th century. In 1860 a temple pavilion was built on the hill, later replaced with a café in 1887. The café was torn down in 1940's. Artificial waterfalls were installed on a slope of *Bastejkalns* already in 1898.

Artificial waterfall cascade in *Bastejkalns*

The House of Blackheads – Destroyed in 1941, Restored in 1999

The House of Blackheads is one of the most splendid buildings of the Rate ("council") Square in Rīga. The busy and vigorous Blackheads who added a touch of glamour to city's social life until 1939 managed the house.

The building of Blackheads was destroyed on June 1941. Its rebuilding was started on June 1996. The stock company *Restaurators* was appointed the responsibilities of the leading building company. Many specialized firms were involved in the complex project, but the most complicated assignments were carried out by specialists from *Restaurators* – construction workers, sculptors, carpenters, blacksmiths, goldsmiths, chandelier designers and other specialists. The new House of Blackheads and Rate Square was inaugurated on the 9th of December 1999. The 7 m high statue of Roland (by sculptor August Folch), the medieval symbol of the city was replaced in the Rate Square same day. The statue was part of the square from 1896 - 1941. Reconstruction of the Rate Square is in progress; reconstruction of Rate House is also planned. The portal of the House of Blackheads is once again furnished with the original inscription:
SOLLT'ICH EINMAL FALLEN NIEDER,
SO ERBRAUET MICH DOCH WIEDER!
("If I'm ever bound to tumble, raise me up again!"), and its door is open to everyone.

The first German carpenters arrived in Rīga in 1202 and settled west of present day *Skārņu* and *Šķūņu ielas*. The market square formed in the 14th century was the beginning of the Rate Square. The medieval Rate Square hosted gatherings on public issues and was enclosed by buildings of public institutions. The House of Blackheads (by Ditrich Kreige) was first mentioned in historic documents in 1334 – Rīga's Rate built the new building on the opposite side of the Rate Square for organisations of merchants and artisans. It was rented out to an organisation of single merchants from Rīga - the Blackheads organisation. Rīga's Blackhead organisation (1416 - 1939) was very influential and wealthy and originated from the Brotherhood of St. George. Mauritius was the patron of the Blackheads; his symbol is displayed on the coat of arms of the organisation.

The House of Blackheads was built in Gothic style suited out as a large medieval dwelling house. It was 27 m high. The house became property of the Blackheads in 1713 and got its present name. The house was rebuilt several times, preserving its Gothic characteristics. The most extensive reconstruction was carried out in 1619 - 1625, when the main facade was rebuilt in North European mannerism, adding the Gothic step pediments, stone decorations, sculptures, ironwork and a clock. There was a ballroom in the House of Blackheads with 12 benches for - Blackheads, Leubeckers, Great Guild, traders of Rīga, Westphalians, etc.

The Latvian National Opera

The Latvian National Opera is located in Rīga, *Aspāzijas bulvāris* 3. The building (1860 – 1863) was built by Henrich Scheel and Fredrich Hehs according to architect Ludwig Bohnstedt design. The main facade, designed in the classical manner, is supported by 6 pillars with allegoric groups of sculptures. The main hall has an ornate Baroque interior. The restoration of opera house lasted several years.

After full restoration of the opera's building in 1995, the theatre launched a new phase of activity. A new generation of performers took their place on the stage in Latvia and throughout Europe. Today Inese Galante, Ingus Pētersons, Egīls Siliņš, Inga Kalna, Aleksandrs Poļakovs are so popular in Europe that they are seen in Latvia only as occasional guests. In the late 1990's colourful performances of *Aida*, *Nabucco*, *Alcina*, *Salome* and other operas with the work of conductors Gintars Rinkēvičs, Aleksandrs Viļumans, as well as director Guntis Gailītis, have become favourites of Rīga's audience and were praised throughout Europe. Many outstanding foreign soloists have been delighted to perform on Rīga's stage.

The tradition of music dates back a long time in Rīga. Opera performances on regular basis have been taking place in Rīga since 1782. Three years after the premiere of Mocart's opera *Flying from Seria* in Vienna, it was performed in Rīga in 1785. Richard Wagner worked in Rīga from 1837 to 1839. Ule Bull, the violinist visited (1838), Franz Lizt (1842), Fiodor Shalapin was here during the peak of his career in 1910. Rīga Opera Chorus assisted Shalapin during his touring in Berlin in 1928.

Valdemārs Komisārs founded Latvian National Ballet in 1918. The royal Vasa order was given to the prima donnas and the director of ballet performance *The Glory of Love* by the Swedish king Gustav VI during a tour in Stockholm in 1935. Ballet dancers Māris Liepa, Michail Barishnikov, Alexander Gudonov, Zita Errsa and other from Latvian school of ballet astonish many in the West. World famous ballet dancers Maya Plisecka, Anna Pavlova and others have performed on the stage of Latvian National Opera. Ballet troupes perform classics like *Swan Lake*, *Bewitched Princess*, *Silfida*, as well as contemporary plays.

The University of Latvia

The building of the University of Latvia was intended for the Rīga Polytechnic, built in 1886. The project was designed by the first dean of the Architecture Department of the Rīga Polytechnic, professor Gustav Ferdinand Alexander Hilbing. The facade is decorated with coats of arms of the three Baltic provinces of Tsarist Russia – Kurzeme, Vidzeme and Estonia. Nine reliefs, drafted by the drawing professor John Clark, are placed above the coats of arms and symbolically portray the specialities taught. Riga Polytechnic was renamed to the Riga Technical Institute in 1896. It was evacuated to Moscow in 1915 during the World War I. On 28 September 1919, the University of Latvia was founded in the building. It has been called the University of Latvia since the academic year 1922/23. It was the major educational, cultural and science centre of Latvia between 1919 and 1940. 30 205 students studied in the university in the academic year 1999/2000.

The oldest university in Latvia is the Rīga Technical University, which was founded in 1862 as a private educational facility with specialities in engineering, chemistry, agriculture, mechanics, trade, land-surveying and agriculture. There are 8 faculties, 30 institutes, 133 professorial groups and several affiliations in other Latvia's cities. The Higher School of Economics, the Academy of Art, the Academy of Culture, the

The building of the University of Latvia in *Raiņa bulvāris* 19, Rīga

University of Ventspils, the University of Vidzeme, the Latvian University of Agriculture, and the *Turība* University play a major part in providing higher education in Latvia.

On 11 April 1997, Latvia and 42 other countries signed the Lisbon Convention on mutual recognition of diplomas from universities of the countries. Latvia, together with the EU countries and associate members of EU has participated in the EU INTAS programmes and several projects of the EUREKA programme since 2000.

Latvian Academy of Art

The Latvian Academy of Art was founded in 1919, commenced activities in 1921, and is located in Rīga, *O. Kalpaka bulvāris* 13. Artists Vilhelms Purvītis, Richards Zariņš, Jānis R. Tilbergs were some of the founders and creators of the academy. Earlier Latvian artists attained professional education in arts in St. Petersburg's Academy of Art (V. Purvītis, Janis Rozentāls, Jānis Valters, and others). The Latvian Academy of Art was created according with the model of St. Petersburg's Academy of Art. After graduating with the basic 4-year curriculum, the right to practice teaching was granted. The advanced curriculum employed 7 studios where the students specialised in selected topics.

Many new talents were discovered with the opening of the Academy of Art; art flourished in Latvia. An expressionistic, Kārlis Padegs, was one of the leading artists in 1920's and 1930's. A sculpture to his honour was placed across the street from the Rīga Latvian Society in *Merķeļa iela*. Gustavs Klucis, one of the world's leading constructionists, learned the basics of art in Rīga. The number of programmes available in the academy has increased in number during the 80 years of its existence. Several generations of artists were educated here and explored their talents after graduation. Some are artists in 2nd and 3rd generation (painters – the Skulmes, Zariņš families).

Alongside with traditional styles of Latvian art, modern styles and ideas are developed and displayed in different installations, projects, etc.

The building of Academy of Art was built in 1905 in architect Vilhelms Bokslaf's design as the Rīga Stock Exchange School of Commerce. The building employs exuberant Neo-gothic forms and is one of the last eclecticism structures in Rīga. The stained glass of windows in stairwells and the main hall were made in Ernests Tode's workshop in Rīga.

Art Nouveau in Riga's Architecture

A. Ļebedenskis' early Art Nouveau apartment house in *Elizabetes iela* 10b, architect M. Eisenstein, 1903

A. Ļebeinskis' apartment house in *Alberta iela* 4, architect M. Eisenstein, 1904, an example to eclectic decorative Art Nouveau

One of the first Art Nouveau buildings in what was once downtown Rīga – a house in *Brīvības iela* 55, 1900, architect V. Neimanis

Art Nouveau has been an outstanding feature of Rīga's image since the late-19th and early-20th century. It is unveiled here in full magnificence. The ornamental aspects of Art Nouveau are best seen on buildings designed by Mikhail Eisenstein in *Alberta iela*, *Elizabetes iela* and *Strēlnieku iela*. Figures of lions and sphinxes are arranged above cornices and facades are decorated with stylistic ornaments of plants, masks, colourful brickwork and ceramic tiles. Many ornate Art Nouveau buildings were built in *Blaumaņa iela*, *Tērbatas iela* and *Rūpniecības iela*. Architects Heinrich Scheel, Karl Felsco, Edmund von Trompovski and others, designed the buildings.

Buildings in rational Art Nouveau style – vertical school – are found in *Brīvības iela*, *Marijas iela* and *Ģertrūdes iela* (architects – Reinhold Schmeling, Wilhelm Bockslaf). Elements of applied arts, inspired by folk art, are characteristic to the national romanticism school of Art Nouveau. The first buildings in this manner (*Marijas iela* 26 and *Tērbatas iela* 15/17) were designed by architects Konstantīns Pēkšēns and Eižens Laube in 1905. The facades of the buildings are modest in decorations; the upper corners of window cases are bevelled, resembling the bent roofs in Latvian folk architecture. Architect Aleksandrs Vanags demonstrates another trend of national romanticism on the buildings in *Brīvības iela*, *A. Čaka iela*, *Lāčplēša iela* and elsewhere. He is consistent in using natural building materials and elements of folklore in facade decor.

VEF

The building of the *Valsts Elektrotehniskā Fabrika – VEF* (State Electrotechnical Factory) in Rīga

Before World War I, the building housed a branch electrotechnical factory of the German stock company *Union*, founded in 1898. The factory produced dynamos, electric motors, and equipment for electric stations and trams. The factory also performed electrification works ordered by railway and manufacturing enterprises. Most of the equipment and workers were evacuated to Kharkov during World War I, where the factory continued its work.

The Main Workshop of Post Telegraphic Central started its work in the building formerly occupied by the *Union* Factory. The workshop was renamed to the State Electrotechnical Factory in 1932.

Several sections of *VEF* building are significant architectural monuments. The administrative section of the former Union Factory was built in 1899 after H. Scheel's design. The assembling section has a metal carcass, metal busbar roof supports, skylights, and an ornate facade built in eclectic manner with a statue of Promethium in the centre. A multi-storied manufacturing building was built in 1912 after P. Behren's design. The building has brick walls, inner metal carcass, reinforced concrete roof supports. The facade is dominated by rational forms. The world's smallest camera, called *Minox* was produced in the factory in 1939. The *VEF* factory was famous throughout the USSR for its radio receivers, telephones, telephone exchanges and other electronic products.

Theatre Museum

The Theatre Museum in Rīga was the house of the famous Latvian director Eduards Smiļģis. The first theatre play in Rīga was performed in 1205, magician shows were often held in medieval Rīga. A permanent German theatre performed in Rīga since 1760. The first theatre play in Latvian was Schiller's *Robbers* performed in *Dikļi* in 1818. Currently 6 professional theatres work in Rīga, including the Russian Drama theatre.

National Museum of Art

The National Museum of Art in Rīga built in 1905 was designed by the famous German architect Wilhelm Neiman. He was also the first director of the museum. Latvian professional art evolved from around the mid-19th century, based on folk art. The first distinguished Latvian artists, the founders of a Latvian art tradition were Kārlis Hūns, Jūlijs Feders, Janis Rozentāls, Vilhelms Purvītis, and Jānis Valters, who received their art education at the St. Petersburg's Academy of Art.

Rīga is a Hospitable City with Cosy and Comfortable Hotels.
There is Nothing Better for a Tourist than a Tour around Vecrīga

Buildings from the 13th – 19th centuries, which were restored in 1995, house the *Konventa sēta* hotel

Park Hotel Rīdzene is surrounded by boulevards. The rooms are nice and cosy, symposiums are often held here. The restaurant in the glass pyramid is modern and attractive

Warehouses in *Vecpilsētas iela* 8a and 10

There is a clock in the very heart of the Rīga city, where people love to arrange rendezvous. It is called the *Laima* clock, which belongs to the confectionery and chocolate factory *Laima*, producer of excellent chocolate candy. *Hotel de Rome* is located across the street from the clock. It is a new and modern hotel, built at the site where the old *Rome Hotel*, which was destroyed by bombing in the war. The *Otto Schwartz* restaurant is located on the top floor of the hotel building. The small open restaurant *Kolonāde* next to the clock is famous for the best pastries in Rīga

Beginning in the second half of the 13th century, masonry buildings were built in the inner yards in Rīga. Warehouses occupied the lower floors and partly the attics of the buildings, while the upper floors were dwelling areas. There were about 128 masonry buildings in *Vecrīga* in the beginning of the 16th century. The development of the transit trade through Rīga during the 17th century required many new masonry buildings for storing grain, hemp products, etc. The warehouses were then built next to residential buildings as close as possible to the *Daugava* and Rīga rivers. There were some 166 storehouses in *Vecrīga* in the end of the 18th century.

The Small Guildhall is located at *Amatu iela* 3/5. It is an architectural monument, built in the mid-14th century. The building was rebuilt several times and the current one was built between 1864 and 1866 on the site of the old building, which was torn down. J. D. Felsco designed the new building.

The Small Guild was transformed from the St. Cross and Trinity Guild, which was founded in the 13th century. It monopolised crafts in cities, because only members of the guild could become artisans. The interior of the building is ornate – there are stained glass windows with coats of arms of the different crafts and portraits of the elders, wall paintings showing city views. The last reconstruction works were carried out in 2000.

The Great Guild was an organisation of German merchants. The basement of the house in *Amatu iela* 6 is all that is preserved from their first building. A two storied building with double nave gathering hall and the *Munster's Room* was built until 1330. The *Bride's Chamber* was added in the 15th century. The present building was built between 1854 and 1857 in K. Beine's architectural design. Architect H. Scheel managed the construction work. The core section with the *Munster's Room* and the *Bride's Chamber* was included in the new building as well. The Great Guildhall is an eclectic building with English Gothic forms and outstanding interior. After a fire in 1963, the building was restored in 1965 to M. Ģelzis' design. A new vestibule was added and the interior was adapted for the performance of concerts.

Concert Life

The Latvian academic choir *Latvia*, which participated in rendering of Giuseppe Verdi's *Requiem* in St. Petersburg in 1997, conducted by the world famous Latvian conductor Mariss Jansons

The choir *Latvia* was founded in 1942, and started its work while still in wartime trenches. It became the most popular choir in Latvia and even outside Latvia during the years that followed. The choir received premiere rendering orders from Edison Denisov (*Requiem*) and Andrew Lloyd Webber (*Requiem*), many awards were won in international competitions. The choir *Latvia*, conducted by Māris Sirmais since 1997, is famous in Europe for the uniquely wide repertoire as well as the refined sound of vocals. Finals of international musical competitions, large events of oratorios and cantatas are held in Rīga, in which choir *Latvia* has a leading role.

Concert life in Latvia at the turn of the 20th and 21st centuries lost its seasonality. Festivals frequently change one another; guests come and go, contests are received with tense interest. Rīga is rich in concert halls each of which has its own acoustics, an image, even its own audience. The most significant concert hall is the Great Guildhall. The National Symphonic Orchestra performs concerts here, mostly symphonic music.

The Radio Latvia choir (conducted by Sigvards Kļava and Kaspars Putniņš), sometimes called the choir with absolute pitch often performs in the Dom Cathedral. The voices of Rīga Dom Boys Choir may also be heard here – the choir has attained recognition in Europe, America and Japan. St. John's Church has good acoustics for vocal and instrumental music. Concerts of chamber music take place in Wagner's Hall, where Richard Wagner once worked. Regular concerts also take place in the hall of *Ave, Sol!* and at the Music Academy on regular basis.

The Dom Cathedral

The Dom Cathedral in *Vecrīga* is the most significant architectural monument in the Baltics from between the 12th and 14th centuries. The largest organ in the world was installed in the cathedral in 1880s. The prospectus of the organ with paintings and carvings in wood was designed by master Jacob Rahb from Gdansk in 1601. Vitreous design is from workshops in Rīga, Munich and Dresden around the turn of the 19th and the 20th century. The chancellery was built in 1641.

The Dom Cathedral served as a concert hall during the Soviet period. Many famous organists have visited and performed here. The unique organ of the Dom Cathedral is known around the world. Rīga Dom Boys Choir is an international award winner. Every visitor to the cathedral will be convinced about the great sound of the organ and the acoustics. The cathedral and its monastery were constructed alongside from 1211 until the second half of the 13th century. The Dom Cathedral was the ideological centre of catholic expansion in Latvia during the Livonian period. The Dom school (founded in 1211) of the monastery educated clerics and was run by the monastery until the Reformation. It was than turned over to city authorities and became the first public institution of higher education.

The building catches attention with its harmonised proportions and a homogenous blend of styles (Romance, Gothic, Baroque, and Classicism). The cathedral is 87 m long, 43 m wide and 26 m high. The courtyard of the monastery is adjacent to the cathedral and enclosed by an arcade gallery on three sides. The 118-m long passage roofed with cross vaults form the 13th century is the only one of the kind in Northern Europe.

The Dom Cathedral was re-established as the cathedral of the Lutheran archbishop in 1991. Both concerts and services take place in the cathedral now.

The Latvian War Cemetery (Brāļu kapi)

The Statue of Mother Latvia in the Latvian War Cemetery in Rīga (sculptor Kārlis Zāle, architects Pēteris Feders and Aleksandrs Birznieks) The Latvian War Cemetery in Rīga is the most distinguished memorial ensemble in Latvia. The cemetery is dedicated to the men who fell during World War I and the Latvian War of Independence. In the nine hectares of the cemetery, there are some 2000 graves of Latvian heroes. The first design of the cemetery was produced in 1915 by architect Eižens Laube. The director of Rīga's parks and gardens at the time, landscape architect Andrejs Zeidaks, designed the non-sculptural parts of the ensemble.

Travertine from the Latvian town of *Ainaži* was selected as the main sculptural material because it would last for centuries. In 1923 the committee, which was set up to organise the project announced a competition for the best sculptural design, and Kārlis Zāle won the competition. Work on the cemetery continued for 12 years. During this time, the landscape was arranged into an architectonic and sculptural ensemble, according to the design by Kārlis Zāle. The memorial ensemble was consecrated on 11 November 1936.

The ensemble is composed of three parts. From the entrance gate people walk along the Path of Reflection, which is 205 m long with linden trees on both sides. The Hero's Terrace with an altar and eternal flame is at the end of the path, and one's view is opened to the area of the graves and the Statue of Mother Latvia and her fallen sons at the other end. In an urn under the sculpture, there are 517 handfuls of earth.– one from each of the 517 parishes, which existed in Latvia at that time.

The Latvian War Cemetery has passed through difficult and complex times. The communists wanted to pull down the Statue of Mother Latvia, but later, in the 1980's buried their own heroes in the cemetery – Soviet military officers.

The Reformed Church

The Reformed Church by architect Christoph Meinart (1727 – 1731) served as a clubhouse during the Soviet period. Later it became a famous disco. The church was returned to the congregation only after reestablishment of the Latvian State

The Lutheran Church of Jesus

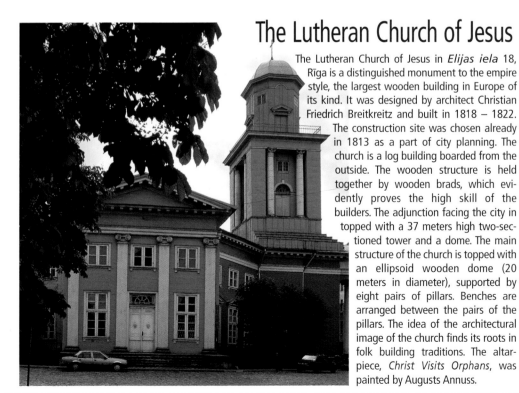

The Lutheran Church of Jesus in *Elijas iela* 18, Rīga is a distinguished monument to the empire style, the largest wooden building in Europe of its kind. It was designed by architect Christian Friedrich Breitkreitz and built in 1818 – 1822. The construction site was chosen already in 1813 as a part of city planning. The church is a log building boarded from the outside. The wooden structure is held together by wooden brads, which evidently proves the high skill of the builders. The adjunction facing the city in topped with a 37 meters high two-sectioned tower and a dome. The main structure of the church is topped with an ellipsoid wooden dome (20 meters in diameter), supported by eight pairs of pillars. Benches are arranged between the pairs of the pillars. The idea of the architectural image of the church finds its roots in folk building traditions. The altarpiece, *Christ Visits Orphans*, was painted by Augusts Annuss.

The Rīga Synagogue

The Rīga Synagogue in *Peitavas iela* 6/8.

Only one synagogue was preserved during the Soviet period in Rīga by a small group of people, which enthusiastically preserved the tradition of Judaism. The religious Jewish circles were once again free to practice their religion and traditions after 1988. Natāns Barkāns became the chief rabbi of Rīga and Latvia.

Jewish people have lived in Latvia for hundreds of years. In the late-19th century in many cities – *Rēzekne, Ludza, Daugavpils* – Jews were half of the total populations. Jews in Latvia were involved in crafts and trade, and many were representatives of the intelligentsia. The democratic system, which existed in the Republic of Latvia from 1918 until 1934, was particularly favourable for the development of Jewish community. World War II was a catastrophe for Jews in Latvia, as in the other countries of Europe that were occupied by the Nazis.

The Jewish contribution to the culture of Latvia was very significant. One of the most distinguished Latvian Jews was the historian Shimon Dubnov, who wrote a 10-volume work on *Jewish world history*. Another distinguished scientist was professor Solomon Hiller, who organised the Organic Synthesis Institute of the Latvian Academy of Sciences and served as its director. The world-famous philosopher Isaiah Berlin, professor at Oxford University was born in Latvia. One of the world's leading sculptors, Naum Aaronson, was born in *Krāslava*, Latvia. The Art Nouveau architect Mikhail Eisenstein was responsible for one of the most outstanding buildings in Rīga – the beautiful house in *Alberta iela* from around the turn of the 19th and 20th centuries. Rīga also contributed two world-class chess players to the world: Arons Nimcovičs and Mihails Tāls. Today many outstanding and talented Jews live and work in Latvia. The revival and development of the Jewish community in Latvia today is a confirmation of the democratic and tolerant attitude in Latvia.

Russian Old Believer Church in Latvia

The Grebenchikov Old believer congregation house in Rīga, *Krasta iela* 73 is an architectural monument, built in 1814 at the location where the old wooden church had burned down two years earlier. The gilded church domes are visible from afar. The main staircase leading to the 2nd floor was added to the original two sections in 1886. Both sections were raised to 4 floors and another three-storied almshouse section was added on the northern side. The Grebenshchikov Church was built in simple Byzantine architectural style. The church tower with the dome (1905 – 1906) has traces of Art Nouveau. There are many icons from the 15th to the 19th century, manuscripts and books from the 16th to the 19th century. Alexander Grebenchikov was a wealthy Russian Old Believer merchant, who donated large amounts of money to the congregation, thus being remembered in the name of both the congregation and its sanctuary.

The Russian Orthodox Church split in the 17th century. Patriarch Nikon made questionable corrections to the book of prayers, ceremonial procedures and symbols. The novelties were not accepted by a part of the religious community, which was, therefore, excommunicated and persecuted. Supporters of the old system were executed on the stake. Many fled to the Baltic region, which was not subject to the control of Russia at the time. The people of Latvia accepted the Russian Old Believer refugees with tolerance. One of the strongest Old Believer communities was established here in the 18th century. There are no historic records of any confrontations between the community and local inhabitants. The Old Believer communities lived by their own social and religious traditions, which secluded them from other religious communities. They were not allowed to smoke, use alcohol or to take meals with the members of other confessions. However, a tolerant attitude towards other confessions is stated in their code of behaviour: *Hold sacred your own traditions; do not make judgments about others*. The Grebenchikov congregation is the largest Old Believer congregation in Latvia and the world.

St. Peter's and St. Paul's Church

The St. Peter's and St. Paul's Church in Rīga is architectural monument, built in early Classicism style. It was built between 1726 and 1728 after the design of Z. Seege von Laurenberg. Its prototype is the Pärnu Orthodox Church (in Estonia). The site was previously occupied by wooden church built during the Swedish era in the 17th century for the needs of citadel's garrison. The construction of a masonry church with a wooden tower was managed by architect K. Haberland, who also designed many details of the church.

The St. Peter's and St. Paul's Church is built in a typical Orthodox manner. The structure resembles a cross. The conjunctive tower is composed of several sections and there is a dome on church's main body, topped with and lantern. The church building is harmonised with the rest of the citadel's main square, and it clearly provides a vertical emphasis to the square. The church was restored in 1987. Restoration was carried out to architect M. E. Mengele's design, which adjusted it to house concerts. Wall and ceiling paintings from the 19th century were preserved and partly restored. The church currently houses the *Ave, sol!* Concert Hall, where concerts by local chamber choirs and guests are held, as well as different cultural events.

The Rīga Hospital No. 7

The Rīga Hospital No. 7 is a part of the health complex *Gaiļezers*, built between 1976 and 1982 after a project by architects Andris Purviņš, Maija and Atis Bīviņš, and others. The composition of the structure is branched. A twelve-storied stationary building is the heart of the complex. The administrative, treatment and educational and other sections branch from the stationary. Pastel colours prevail in the high quality interior. The *Gaiļezers* hospital complex is one of the most modern health treatment facilities built in Europe in 1970's.

Roads in Latvia

The quality of roads is kept up with the level of world standards not only in Rīga, but also in the rest of Latvia. The Rīga – *Jūrmala* and Rīga – *Sigulda* dual carriageways are modern highways with proper access roads, viaducts and information. Road traffic safety is an important concern and the carriageways are secluded from each other. All the highways and most first-class roads

The *Salu* (Island) Bridge is a major traffic bypass

are equipped with road signs and information in line with international standards. *Signum* factory produces road signs and other equipment not only for Latvia, but also for export. Roadway markings are in place on all main and first-class roads, as well as plastic signal posts with reflectors and barriers to keep careless drivers on the road.

The development and maintenance of international co-operation has made the decision-making process easier at the different levels of road management. Contacts have helped to increase understanding of trends of development in the field, raised the qualifications of Latvian road engineers and specialists, provided information and experience in dealing with the latest technologies and methods.

The system of financing and managing Latvia's road network has been recognised as one of the most progressive and promising in Europe. The Latvian Roads Directorate continues to actively co-operate in five international roads organisations – the *Baltic Road Workers Council*, the *World Roads Association*, the *International Roads Federation*, the *International Association of Bridge Constructors and Engineers*, and the *Nordic Roads Association*. In 1998, the three Baltic States and Finland launched a joint project to develop a Baltic region highway and a system of meteorological information stations. Work on the *Via Baltica* highway, which will run from Helsinki to Warsaw, and its associated infrastructure development is also continuing.

The Largest Market in Europe.
The 368 m High Television Tower

Rīga's Central Market is the largest marketplace in Europe. There are separate pavilions for meat products, milk products, vegetables, fish, pastries covering an area of 14 000 m^2. There are also two sheds with a total area of 4.7 thousand m^2. There are 94 stands selling hardware and commodities. There is also a market square. About 5000 selling stands are spread over a total area of 87.8 thousand m^2. About 100 000 customers make purchases every day in the market. The unique Rīga's Central Market is an object of interest to every visitor of the city, even royalty and famous artists.

The construction of Rīga's Central Market was carried out between 1924 and 1930 in Pāvils Dreimanis and Pāvils Pavlovs design. Brickwork was done by Russian Old Believer bricklayers from Latgale. The foundations of the sales halls are made out of reinforced concrete. The buildings on the market have brick walls and arched metallic busbar roofs arranged over the Zeppelin hangar structures from World War I. The largest pavilion (5000 m^2) – the meat produce one – was initially reserved for the wholesale trade. All the pavilions have basements. Underground tunnels with exits at the canal connect the pavilions. The system is convenient for delivering goods to storehouses and freezers. The pavilions are well lit, ventilated and heated.

Windmill in Krasta Iela – a New, High Quality Restaurant with More than 1000 Seats

A new complex of restaurants and recreation, nicknamed *Kirson's windmill* by the people, stands out and catches one's eye as one drives along the highway of *Krasta iela*. It invites one for a closer look, and tempts one to relax and try *Lido's* cuisine. Once you surrender yourself to do so, you will do it without hesitation next time. Parking is convenient here in the parking lots, which are arranged in terraces on different levels of artificial elevation. The windmill is a functioning object with working wings. The visual appearance of the building employs elements of modern architecture. The method of corner-joined construction is applied to a great extent, so are other methods and elements observed in rural settlements. The combination of effects on the facade produces an appearance of a monumental structure. Elements of folklore are abundant on the rear of the building – clay bricks and boulders. A successful combination of granite pavement in the lobby and staircase, walls and bent sliding doors in glass characterise the main entrance. The passage to

the bellow stairs runs under a boulder overhang. The granite washing-table and the low ceiling with vault imitations are impressive with the quality of design. The ground floor is a large and light hall occupied by a restaurant. There is a separate hall in the windmill tower with stained glass windows, an elevation around the centre of the tower, naturally tilted wooden fences and a long counter for the open kitchen. The upstairs have simple, yet spectacular wall construction, which merges with the roof support illuminated by a pillar of falling, boat-shaped light visible even from below stairs.

The interior is furnished with copies in 1930's design, a presence of tested values. The wooden tables of the below stairs are decorated with paintings of famous politicians and artists. The total area of the complex is 2.8 hectares, the building occupies an area of 6993 m^2, and it has more than 1000 seats. The architect of the complex is Andris Puriņš. The project was completed in 1999.

Clubs and Restaurants Are Open 24-hours a Day Every Day of the Week in Rīga Providing Great Opportunities for Rectreation and Leisure

Nourishing and appetising meals have always been highly valued in Latvia. Already since the 19th century Rīga restaurants have attracted local people and their guests. There are a number of restaurants in Rīga that are open 24 hours a day and comply with the most refined taste.

S/C *Admirāļu klubs* has been working already for 10 years. Its name is well – known in the whole country and it is a guarantee of high level service.

Gourmands of Rīga and their guests enjoy the biggest restaurant – variety show in the Baltic States – the *Grand Cabare Admiral*, which is situated at *Blaumaņa iela* 32, Rīga. It is luxurious, classical, with rich and versatile choice of food and exclusive show program. It is the only show – program in the Baltic States, which corresponds to the best traditions of classical variety shows. Excellent service helps to create a special atmosphere for pleasant recreation. From the restaurant you can go to a European level casino with card tables, roulette tables and updated game machines of European make.

With its 3 casino halls, 50 game machine halls and 15 billiards halls S/C *Admirāļu klubs* is one of the biggest companies in the entertainment industry in Latvia. S/C *Admirāļu klubs* offers different billiards tables produced by the best European companies. You can purchase billiard accessories, casino game tables and game machines at the shop *Spēļu paradīze*, situated at *Skolas iela* 14, Rīga.

The Port of Rīga

The Port of Rīga is Latvia's largest in terms of territory. It handles three-quarters of the cargo that is transhipped through Latvia. The Port of Rīga can handle a variety of freight, except for crude oil. The majority of cargo at this time consists of wood products, mineral fertilisers, metals, containers and oil products. Since 1996, the port's annual turnover has increased by an average of 7% per year. The main advantage of the port is its favourable geographic location and the highly developed network of road and rail transport that accesses the port. 80% of all the cargo that is loaded at the Port of Rīga is transit cargo.

The law on the Free Port of Rīga provides a variety of benefits to companies that work in the territory of the port, including customs, excise and value added tax relief. By 2010, investments in the Port of Rīga will be made to an amount of more than 100 million lats, and the money will be used to rebuild existing piers and to build new piers. Shipping in winter depends on ice conditions in the Gulf of Rīga and the *Irbe* Strait. On the relatively rare occasions, when the bay freezes over, icebreakers are available.

There were piers in the Old Rīga Port as early as the 12th century. 20-m wide piers supported by oak tree logs were built in the 13th century as an extension of fortification walls. It was used as a winter port and a pier until the 18th century. As the *Daugava* River often changed its riverbed and depth, it started to be artificially guided in 1764. The appearance of the first steamboats encouraged new construction works in the Port of Rīga. In the 19th century additions to the port were also built at *Vecmīlgrāvis* and *Bolderāja*, piers were built on *Andrejsala* and a lighthouse at the mouth of the river. The Exports port was started in the early-20th century. The part of the Port of Rīga upstream from the bridges is relatively shallow, and therefore it was mostly used for flooding logs - up to 15 000 rafts could be handled at a time. *Mīlgrāvis* was another log port. Rīga was the largest log port in the world. The current in the lower *Daugava* River is too weak to carry silt out and it deposits at the mouth of the river. The necessary depth is maintained with the help of machinery. Major deepening work was done in 1930's, when the whole of *Uzvara* square was covered in sand from the bottom of the *Daugava* River, and 10 m high stacks of silt were placed between *Slokas iela* and *Dārtas iela* and *Raņķis* dam. The Irbe Strait and the Port of Rīga can currently handle *Panamax*-type ships with a loaded weight of 50 000 tons and above.

Russian tsars were especially interested in construction of *Daugavgrīvas* breakwater and the Port of Rīga. Stone plates on *Daugavgrīvas* breakwater were dedicated to their annual visits

Timber Export

The most notable achievement of Latvian timber industry during the last 10 years is the very rapidly increasing export to West Europe. *Linda Grupa* is a timber industry concern, which rents 28 hectares of land in the territory of the free port of Rīga, and realises the largest shipping project of timber in the Baltic States.

The annual capacity of the port is gradually increasing. New truck and train accommodation roads will be built. The specialised terminal for timber export makes the process of loading faster and fulfils the necessary requirements for storing and loading of the cargo. It also attracts timber transit from Russia and Belarus, thus contributing to the State budget through taxes and tolls.

The timber industry accounts for about 38% of Latvia's exports, which may be explained with the good condition of Latvia's forests and the high quality of the timber. Latvian undertakings began as early as 1991, and the high quality of their product, precision-made work and good organisation quickly lived up to the EU standards. *Nelss* Ltd. supplies 8 – 10% of the timber construction market of Great Britain. The most profitable way to use Latvian birch trees is in plywood manufacturing. Plywood production is mostly exported to 35 countries, and most of it goes to Great Britain, Germany, Netherlands, and Denmark. The port of Rīga also handles sawn materials and other timber exports.

Liepāja

St. Anna's Church was first mentioned in historical documents in 1509, rebuilt on sereral occasions. Fully restored after a project by architect Paul M. Berci in 1893

St. Trinity Church in *Lielā ielā* 7

Liepāja is Latvia's third largest city, sometimes called *Jūras vārti* (Sea Gates), and is located between the Baltic Sea and the *Liepājas* and *Tosmāras* lakes. *Liepāja* obtained the rights of a city in 1625. It was first mentioned in historical documents on 1253. *Liepāja* is rich in significant historical and cultural monuments, art and cultural heritage. This is the site of the outstanding religious and architectural monuments of Prussia, the St. Trinity Lutheran Church (designed by Johann Dorn, 1742 – 1758), the St. Anne's Lutheran Church with the famous altar produced by the distinguished wood carver, Sefrens Junior in 1697. The church was mentioned in historical documents already in 1509, but it was built at its present location after a design by architect Paul Bertschy in 1893. There are many buildings in *Liepāja* by the architect.

In the 13th century, the site that is now occupied by *Liepāja* was the location of a Liv fishing port and a village. The *Liepāja* port was built between 1697 and 1703, and then extended between 1860 and 1904. During the latter period there were 70 – 80 ships registered at the port, and there was regular steamboat traffic with all the Baltic Sea ports in Russia and Germany, as well as Scandinavia. *Liepāja's* development has always been dictated entirely by economic considerations – first the port, then the expanded industrial activity. In 1899, *Liepāja* became the first city in Eastern Europe to boast an electric tram. The *Green Pharmacy* in *Liepāja* served as an example for Russia's first 100 pharmacies – each of which was a precise copy of the pharmacy in *Liepāja*. There are 47 educational institutions in *Liepāja*, Latvia's oldest symphony orchestra, and a city theatre. The city is the site of a traditional rock festival, *Liepājas Dzintars* (*Liepāja* Amber) and has an ice hall where Latvia's national ice-hockey team – one of the top ten teams in the world – holds its training sessions.

The Port of Liepāja

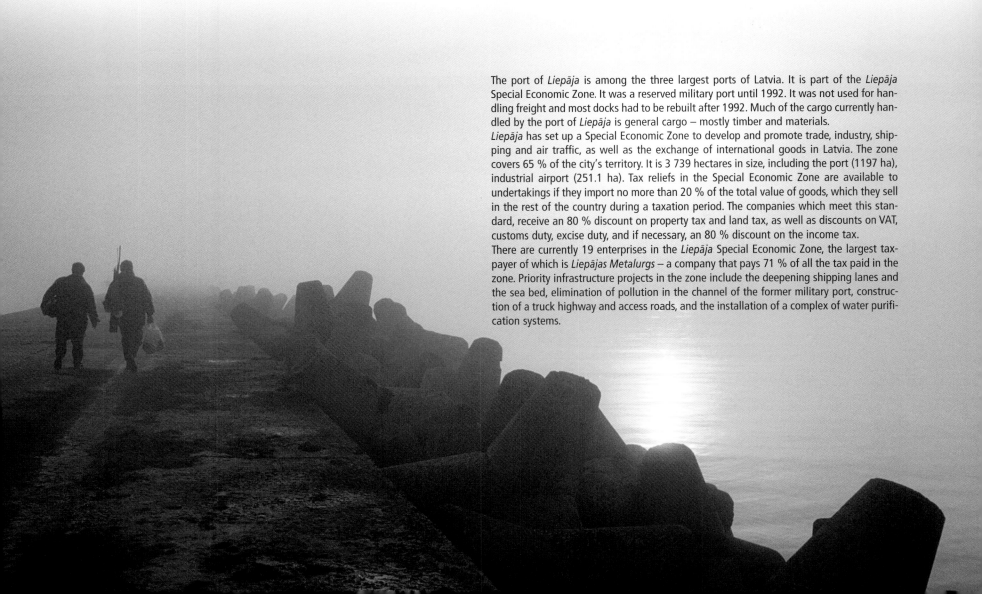

The port of *Liepāja* is among the three largest ports of Latvia. It is part of the *Liepāja* Special Economic Zone. It was a reserved military port until 1992. It was not used for handling freight and most docks had to be rebuilt after 1992. Much of the cargo currently handled by the port of *Liepāja* is general cargo – mostly timber and materials.

Liepāja has set up a Special Economic Zone to develop and promote trade, industry, shipping and air traffic, as well as the exchange of international goods in Latvia. The zone covers 65 % of the city's territory. It is 3 739 hectares in size, including the port (1197 ha), industrial airport (251.1 ha). Tax reliefs in the Special Economic Zone are available to undertakings if they import no more than 20 % of the total value of goods, which they sell in the rest of the country during a taxation period. The companies which meet this standard, receive an 80 % discount on property tax and land tax, as well as discounts on VAT, customs duty, excise duty, and if necessary, an 80 % discount on the income tax.

There are currently 19 enterprises in the *Liepāja* Special Economic Zone, the largest taxpayer of which is *Liepājas Metalurgs* – a company that pays 71 % of all the tax paid in the zone. Priority infrastructure projects in the zone include the deepening shipping lanes and the sea bed, elimination of pollution in the channel of the former military port, construction of a truck highway and access roads, and the installation of a complex of water purification systems.

Ventspils – the Largest Port on the Coasts of the Baltic Sea

Ventspils is the largest exporter of oil products in the Baltic Sea region, a modern European
city and an ice free port, which has become an important link of transit between the East and the West.
Since 1997, *Ventspils* has had free port status. The stock company *Ventbunkers* reloads various types of oil products,
forwards cargoes, loads ships and provides other services. The stock company *Ventamonjaks* is one of the largest
chemicals reloading terminals on the Baltic Sea. The terminal handles ammonia and 12 other liquid chemicals and
oil chemistry products. The company handles 1.8 million tons of products each year. *Ventamonjaks* has three deep-
water piers and storage tanks with a capacity of 200 000 m^3. The stock company *Kālija parks* is the world's largest
terminal for the reloading of potassium salt. The warehouse space of *Kālija parks* is 115 000 tons with room for up
to six different fertilisers. In the second half of 1999 a new 280 – meter pier with a depth of 15.5 m was opened. It
has a ship-loading machine that can handle 3000 tons per hour.
Ventspils was first mentioned in historical documents in 1263 under the name of the port of *Vinda*. In 1290, a stone
castle was built, and the city was a member of the Hanseatic League between the 14th and 16th centuries. In the
17th century, it was an important port for the Dukedom of Kurzeme - a centre for shipbuilding and trade. The strongest
impulse for the development of the city came when a railroad line was open between *Ventspils* and Ribinska.
There are about 50 000 residents, it has the highest rate of employment and highest average wage in Latvia. More
than 1700 companies and enterprises are registered in *Ventspils*. Many changes have been introduced to the city
during the last ten years. There is a university in the city, as well as affiliates of other institutions for higher educa-

tion. Various international
cultural events take place in
Ventspils. Residents and
guests of the city have every
opportunity to practice
sports in modern sports facilities. The old part of the city
has been restored, parks and
the seashore have been
brought into order, and
streets have been paved. The
Ventspils castle – an architectural monument from the
13th century has been
restored. The city government has created favourable
conditions for improving and
restoring privately owned
buildings as well.

Ventspils Nafta (Ventspils Petroleum)

The stock company *Ventspils Nafta* is one of the largest terminals for oil and oil products in the Baltic Sea region. It covers an area of 100 hectares, the combined storing capacity of oil tanks is over one million cubic meters.

The company with 40 years of experience developed rapidly into the most modern and promising undertaking in the Baltic States in 1990's. Its major advantages are the favourable geographic location at an ice free port, developed infrastructure, huge capacity and experience. Oil is transported from Russia via pipeline, oil products come by rail from Russia, while diesel fuel is piped in from Russia, Lithuania and Belarus. The company also unloads gasoline from tankers and loads into railroad cisterns and tanker trucks. Oil and oil products from *Ventspils* are mostly exported to Western Europe and North America.

The oil tanks and tank parks as well as the necessary equipment used therein are the most up-to-date in the Baltic Sea region. The tank park has two rail trestles for the loading and unloading of oil products from railroad cars, technological pumping stations and other important ancillary services. After the reconstruction of the port and a deepening of the shipping channel, SC *Ventspils Nafta* can now service ships with weight up to 120 000 tons – the largest of the ships that can enter the Baltic Sea. Today it is common to see two or three ships at a time at SC *Ventspils Nafta*, which carry 100 000 tons or more each. This has increased the competitiveness of SC *Ventspils Nafta* quite considerably, allowing freight owners to reduce shipping costs.

The transit corridor of SC *Ventspils Nafta* has become cheaper by approximately USD 15 million per year thanks to the deepening of the port. SC *Ventspils Nafta* is expanding and modernising its operations in line with international standards, both in terms of client service and environmental protection. The company's environmental and quality management system has been certified on the basis of the ISO-9002 and ISO-14001 standards.

Daugavpils

Daugavpils is the second largest city in Latvia and the main centre of the Latgale region. The city is located on the right bank of the *Daugava* River, between the river and Lake *Stropi*. *Daugavpils* is the only city in the world in which one can stand in one place and see the churches of all four of Latvia's major christian confessions - the Lutherans, the Roman Catholics, the Orthodox and the Old Believers. St. Peter's Church, which is owned by the Catholics, as well as the Lutheran Church in the city, were built by the architect Wilhelm Naumann. The Lutheran Church suffered heavy damage during World War II. After the war the church was confiscated by the Soviet government and used as a warehouse. The largest Orthodox church in the city is the St. Boris Gleb Orthodox Cathedral. The St. Neva Alexander Cathedral, which was built in the mid-19th century, was torn down in a single night during the 1950's.

Daugavpils is an important transportation hub. Railway lines connect the city to Rīga, Vilnius, St. Petersburg, Kaunas and Šauliai. There are nine lakes in the city. The iron bridge across the *Daugava* River was built in 1853.

Daugavpils has a very varied population. In the 18th century, many non-Latvians settled in the vicinity. In 1897, in fact, only 1.8 % of the city's population was ethnic Latvian – The remainder were Jewish, Russian, Polish, Lithuanian, etc. Even today only 14.2 % of the 117.5 thousand residents are ethnic Latvians.

Daugavpils was first mentioned as a settled area in the 5th century, when people from the island of Gottland sailed up the *Daugava* River to Russia and later – to Greece. The Livonian Order began to build a stone castle of Dinaburg in 1275. Many armies from different countries have crossed the city, it was destroyed and rebuilt many times. Its name was often changed – Dinaburg, Borisoglebsk, Dvinsk, *Daugavpils*. *Daugavpils* does not have what would be called old town. The oldest part of the city is around the *Daugavpils* fort from the 19th century. When work on the fort began in 1810, many old buildings were torn down or moved.

There is a theatre and a zoo in *Daugavpils*. The *Daugavpils* Pedagogical University and a branch of the Rīga Technical University are to be found in the city.

Manufacturing is well developed in *Daugavpils* – locomotive repair shops, large facilities for textile manufacturing and the manufacture of chemicals.

Jelgava

Academia Petrina

The building of *Academia Petrina* in *Jelgava*, located in *Akadēmijas iela* 10. It now houses the Ģ. Elias Museum of *Jelgava's* History and the Museum of Art

Jelgava was the capital of Dukedom of Kurzeme and now is an important centre for culture and education in Latvia. The region where *Jelgava* is now located was populated in the 2nd millennium BC. The city of *Jelgava* was mentioned in documents for the first time in 1265, when the Livonian Order started to build a wooden castle here. *Jelgava* was granted the rights of a city in 1573, and five years later the Duke of Kurzeme moved here. After the Northern War, the city grew quickly into a major centre for crafts and trade. In 1738, Duke Ernst Johann Biron started to build the *Jelgava* castle, which today is the most important architectural monument in the city. *Academia Petrina* of *Jelgava* was opened in 1775 and became a major contributor to the development of science in Latvia. The name of Ernest Bihneman, student of the academy, is connected with the first air-balloon flights in *Jelgava*. The Russia tsar Pavil ordered that the academy be made into university in 1800 and to move it to *Tērbata* (Tartu, Estonia) in 1802.

The city suffered extensive damage during World War II, with the Russian bombing the city as intensively as the Allies bombed Dresden. After the war, *Jelgava* was the site of various industries, and it became Latvia's fourth major industrial centre. The *RAF* factory that produced 10-seat passenger vans and ambulances for the entire Soviet Union was also opened.

Today *Jelgava* is a student city. The Latvian University of Agriculture is here since 1939, as well as a People's University, the Zemgale Business School and the Adult Education Centre. Interesting historical exhibitions are displayed in the *Jelgava* Museum of History and the *Jelgava* palace.

The Jelgava Palace

The *Jelgava* palace is an architectural monument of state importance. Construction of the palace was started in 1738 at the location of the old Livonian Order castle. Ernst J. Biron had become the Duke of Kurzeme one year earlier. His dream was a large, ornate palace in the metropolis of the dukedom, *Jelgava*. Space for the palace was created by blasting the old Livonian Order castle, the seat of the Duke Ketler dynasty in 1737. Biron was even more interested in *Jelgava* than *Rundāle*, and some of the building materials prepared for *Rundāle* were transferred to *Jelgava* – parquet, stoves, etc.

The palace was built according to Francesco Bartolomeo Rastrelli's design. The foundations were laid, the structure was built in Baroque style and building materials for the interior were prepared until 1740. A palace coup d'etat took place in Russian court. Biron was arrested and sent into exile, putting a halt to construction work. It continued only in 1763 after Biron returned to Kurzeme. Rastrelli also returned to *Jelgava*, but this time the construction work was managed by Danish architect Severin Jensen, adding a touch of

Classicism to the building. A guest sculptor from Berlin, Johan Michael Graf, worked here between 1768 and 1774 and an Italian painter, Antonio d'Angeli – between 1768 and 1771. The court moved into the palace in 1772.

The famous Kaliostro spent some time in the *Jelgava* palace in 1779. Louis XVIII, exiled by the French Revolution, stayed in the *Jelgava* palace in 1798. He arrived together with the queen, the family, and the court, escorted by many French emigrants. The large Ballroom was divided into many separate rooms. Furniture was brought from St. Petersburg. Never had the *Jelgava* palace hosted so many prominent and ornate quests. Cardinal Monmoransi wedded the grandson of Duke of Angulema with the daughter of Louis XVI, Maria Teresa Charlotte on 30 May 1799. The king went to Warsaw on January 1800, returned to *Jelgava* in 1804 and left for good in 1807. Napoleon's army established a war hospital in the *Jelgava* palace. The palace survived many wars and was renovated several times. It currently houses the Latvian University of Agriculture.

Jūrmala – Ecologically Clean Beach with Good Opportunities for Recreation

Latvia's resort city of *Jūrmala* is located on the shores of the Gulf of Rīga. It covers an area of 100 square km. There are 58.8 thousand residents in the multicultural city.
The natural beauty of the city is, of course, connected with the sea. Pine forests cover the coastal areas and natural forests are found around *Dzintari*, *Vaivari* and *Valteri*. There are also birches, asps and broad-leaved trees around *Ķemeri*, many parks and gardens are found in the city. The *Ķemeri* scenery park is an outstanding landmark, which was started in the mid-19th century.
The beach area covers a total of 176 hectares. Just as the beaches are rather flat, the sea is shallow and one may wade from one sandbar to another far into the water. Destructive storms are quite rare. The waves are rarely higher than 1–2 m. There have been problems with pollution during the last few years. The solution of salt is very low – 0.5 to 0.7%. The swimming season lasts from June to early September. There is an average of 1500 sunny hours per year in *Jūrmala*. October is the rainiest month of the year. Temperature reaches a maximum of +24° to +28°C in July and August. Winters are warmer here than they are in the mainland, -4C on average. Water temperature in summer months is +19.5° to +24°C, and the sea cools down much slower than the air. Air pollution has been reduced significantly during the last few years due to limitations on road transports through the city.
The present day territory of *Jūrmala* became a major resort for swimming in the 19th century. Rīga and *Jūrmala* were connected with a scheduled traffic of dirigibles in 1824 and steamboats in 1844. The *Melluži* recreation facility is open since 1827. A hotel with a main hall for up to 300 persons and four more recreation facilities were built in 1847. The city received more than 3000 guests in 1845. *Jūrmala* was a popular resort centre with a well-developed network of rehabilitation and recreation facilities during the first period of Latvian independence (1918 – 1940). During the Soviet occupation, *Jūrmala* was the best-known resort in the entire Soviet Union. The tourist flow from the East reduced after the renewal of Latvia's independence. *Jūrmala* is reclaiming its prestigious role as a resort city over the last few years. The number of people seeking relaxation and recreation opportunities is increasing. Several health resorts have been reopened. The rehabilitation centre *Vaivari* has acquired much popularity.

The Hotel *Majori* in *Jomas iela* 29, City of *Jūrmala*.

The hotel was built in 1925, designed by German architect Arthur Medlinger (1880 – 1961). The construction was managed by Jēkabs Paeglis. The building is a classic example to eclectic architecture with elements of neo-classicism and neo-Baroque. The composition is a demonstration of the, so-called family *Heimat style*

Kuldīga

The *Alekšupīte* River with buildings right next to water meanders through *Kuldīga*, which then resembles a *little Venice*. The 4.15 m high *Alekšupīte* waterfall is the highest in Kurzeme and the second highest in Latvia. It is located near a water mill from the 13th century.

Kuldīga has an urban environment, which was created by artisans, merchants and craftsmen. It is the only city in Latvia where large and unchanged streets of wooden buildings from the 18th and the 19th centuries are still preserved. Narrow streets and red tiling roofs are characteristic of the city. A 165-m long bridge across the *Venta* River is located in *Kuldīga*. Carved boulders support the bridge, and the spans are built in brick. *Ventas Rumba*, the widest (110 m) waterfall in Latvia, is here as well. It is 2 m high.

Bendes Namiņš ("the hangman's house") – the guard's house of the castle stands on the left bank of the *Venta* River. Legends tell that the hangman lived here in medieval times. The name of *Kuldīga* first appeared in historical documents in 1245, when Bishop Wilhelm decreed that Kurzeme would be part of Prussia. The largest and most powerful Kurish castle was once here. The Jesusburg castle, later called the Goldingen castle, was built here in 1242 – 1245. The region populated by Kurish tribes along the *Venta* and *Abava* rivers was an important object of international interest in the 13th century. In 1378, *Kuldīga* was granted the right of a city, and in 1398, it joined the Hanseatic League.

Kuldīga is home to the St. Catherine's Lutheran Church, where the altar and chancel, created by wood sculptor Sefrenss the Elder, date back to 1660 – 1663, while the pipe organ, produced by K. Raneus, dates back to 1712 – 1715. Both are architectural monuments of global importance.

Main employers of the work force in the city today include automobile repair, wood processing, transportation, and service companies. There are affiliates of the Rīga College of Education and Educational Management of the *Liepāja* Pedagogical Academy in the city.

Talsi

Talsi is one of the most spectacular of Latvia's cities – it is built on nine lakeside hills. Highway A10 Rīga – *Ventspils* runs 4 km south of the city's frontiers

The city was first mentioned in historical documents in 1231. *Talsi* was conquered by the Livonian Order in 1253. The city suffered great damage during the Polish-Swedish war and the Northern War. It flourished only in the 19th century. Talsi was given limited self-government in 1894. A group of Tsarist government militia torched 60 buildings during the revolution of 1905. There is a monument to the revolutionaries of 1905 on the *Leču* Hill. The *Punishment Pine* preserves the memory of the 5 revolutionaries shot here in 1906.

The historical centre of *Talsi* is located on the shores of Lake *Talsu*. The most beautiful street in *Talsi* is *Lielā iela* – several buildings from the 19th century are preserved here. *Talsi* is the only place where gable ridge roofs with downward sloped edges are seen on buildings. The *Ķēniņkalns* (King Hill) on the banks of Lake *Talsu* is about 500 m long, 100 m wide and 3 m high. A legend tells that a king was buried underneath it, and people brought dirt in

their hats to build the hill. There is a park on the hill with the monument *Koklētājs* (the kokle player) by Kārlis Zemdega dedicated to Latvian freedom fighters of the War of Independence; it was restored in 1996. There are many stairways in *Talsi* connecting hills and valleys. The summer manor of Baron von Fircks, built between 1883 and 1885, is an outstanding architectural monument, and today it houses the local museum. *Talsi* is also the site of a pharmacy that first opened its doors in 1787 and is still working today. The altarpiece *Kristus debesbraukšana* (Christ's Ascension) by an artist from Dresden, K. Schenhart, as well as stained glasswork and church bells (1601) are found in *Talsi* Church. A printing house, companies that produce construction materials and build roads provide the main employment in *Talsi*. The food processing industry is developing in the city as well.

Kandava

The stone bridge across the *Abava* River was built in 1873 ordered by Baron von Fircks. It is one of the oldest stone bridges in Latvia. The bridge is 66 m long. There are stone obelisks, which once supported stone plates with dates and the name of Baron von Fircks on both sides in the middle of the bridge. The plates were taken away in the beginning of 1960's. *Kandava* is a city in the valley of the *Abava* River in Kurzeme, sometimes called the *Switzerland of Kurzeme*, is one of the most beautiful towns in Latvia. *Kandava* (*Candowe*) means *a place next to water* in Liv.

The Kurs had a castle at what is now called *Kandava* between the 10th and the 12th centuries. The name of the city appeared in historical documents for the first time in 1230. The Livonian Order took over *Kandava* in 1253 and built a castle there. Although the city flourished and became a major trading centre for the surrounding region during the 17th century, the full rights of a city were awarded to *Kandava* only in 1917.

Kandava is interesting because of its early 20th century architecture, however, the oldest buildings from the 18th century are found around the market square and ones from the 19th century in *Lielā iela* and *Talsu iela*. There is a synagogue, built in Roman style in the early 20th century in *Kandava*. The most important building monument is a four-arch bridge across the *Abava* River, which was built at the suggestion of Baron von Fircks on an open field, after which the flow of the river was diverted. The site of the former castle still has a square tower with walls that are two meters thick. During the reign of Duke Jacob of Kurzeme, gunpowder was stored in the tower and it is known as the Powder Tower to this very day.

Two wooden sculptural groups are preserved in the *Kandava* Lutheran church (1730 – 1736) – the *Malefactor* and *Golgotha* (17th century) and the altarpiece *Jesus on the Cross* by K. Arnoldi (1860). The city is known for its cleanliness and order. The *Second Three-star sports games* took place in *Kandava* in 1997. Development of sports industry is planned in the future as well.

Alūksne

The Lutheran Church of *Alūksne* (to the left), built in 1781 – 1788, and Glück's Bible museum (to the right)

Alūksne is one of the most beautiful and unique Latvian cities in the region often called *Malēnija*. Latvians tell many jokes about *Malēnians*; how a *Malēnian* carries light in a strainer, or pushes a log up on a hill only to roll it down to where he started from. It seems like the jokes are made up by the *Malēnians* themselves. The ability to laugh at oneself is a sign of vitality and spiritual exuberance, characteristic to people from *Alūksne* who love their traditions. People of *Alūksne* are known for their large gatherings in *Alūksne* during the All Saints festival at the end of summer. People pay respect to their ancestors and strengthen their sense of unity, then they return to their everyday business, cherish and develop their city. Its history is filled with ancient testimonies.

The oldest Latgallian settlement and castle was found in what is now called *Templa* Hill. German Crusaders burnt down the Latgallian castle in 1225. Swedes and Russians have plundered the city as well. Sheremetjev's army besieged *Alūksne* in 1702. Many citizens were taken captive, among them the Rev. Ernest Glück and his foster child Marta Skavrovska (Vārna), who later came to be the Russian Empress Catherine I.

E. Glück played a significant role in the history of *Alūksne*. In 1685 he completed the translation of the Old Testament into Latvian and in 1689 – the New Testament. In honour of each of the translations, he planted an oak tree, which are now called the *Glück Oaks*. There is a Glück's Bible museum in *Alūksne* now. Nothing but ruins are left of the Livonian Order castle. The ensemble of *Alūksne's* estate was built in the Classical style during the 18th and the 19th century.

The new castle of *Alūksne* is a monument to Neo-gothic style. Its park contains a variety of shapes and mythological ancient Greek sculptures. The castle stands of the banks of Lake *Alūksne*. The lake is 6 km long, 4.3 km wide and 15.2 m deep. There are several islands in the lake: *Cepurīte*, *Pilssala*, *Garā* and *Tīklu* islands.

Strenči

Strenči is located in the *Tālava* lowlands, *Sedas* plains. There is a 5 km section of rapids starting form *Strenči* and downstream on the *Gauja* River. A tributary of the *Gauja* River called the *Strenčupīte* River runs through the town. The large *Sedas* swamp starts north-east of the town. The town covers an area of 5.7 square km and it has almost 2 000 permanent residents. In 1928 the rights of a town were granted to *Strenči*. The town has centuries long traditions as a timber centre, it was once settled by lumbermen and rafters of the *Gauja* River. Rafters' celebrations take place in *Strenči* every year.

The State Psychiatric hospital was founded here in 1907. The architect A. Reinbergs designed the building. The first stage of construction was started in 1904. Two and three storied brick buildings are spread out and arranged on a large plot of land. The environment of the hospital park is harmonised and pleasant to the eye. The psychiatric hospital at *Strenči* provided the best treatment available in Russia and even Europe. In 1943, the Nazis killed the patients, who were not taken from the hospital by their relatives during the war.

The development of the city came to a halt after the war. *Strenči* was the only town in Latvia, where no new buildings were built after the war until 1996, when a sewage plant and a pipeline network for hot water supply were built, organised by the Ministry of Environmental Protection and Regional Development in co-operation with colleagues from Denmark.

The *Strenči* Lutheran Church is an example to non-traditional architecture – it has elements of Art Nouveau. The altarpiece is by I. Zeberiņš – *Christ and Peter at the Ocean* (1957).

A pharmacy was opened here in 1901, and it still works today. The town festival has been celebrated in *Strenči* every August since 1995.

Aizpute

Aizpute is one of the oldest towns in Latvia. Archaeological evidence proves the area was populated as early as the 2nd – 4th century. The fortified *Beida* Kurish castle, also called the *Asenputte* castle was located on the right bank of the *Tebra* River by the Rīga – Prussia trade and war route. The Livonian Order built the castle of the bishop of the Domkapitul near the Kurish castle in 1248, in the 13th century. Later it became the administrative centre of *Piltene* district. *Aizpute* attained the rights of a city in 1378.

Aizpute is currently an important centre for art, culture, history and architecture. The city planning is typical of the 13th to 19th centuries, wooden buildings are still preserved. The most significant architectural monuments are the Livonian Order castle ruins and the Lutheran church. The manufacturing enterprise *Kurzemes Atslēga 1* is located in *Aizpute*. Road repair and food processing industries develop in the town as well.

Smiltene

Smiltene is a town in the Vidzeme highlands, surrounded by beautiful parks and greenery. *Smiltene* attained the rights of a city in 1920. It covers an area of 7.19 square km, the population is 6413 residents, and 93.6% of them are ethnic Latvians.

Three sand dunes are visible on the coat of arms of the town, although there are actually about seven of them. There are roads heading in seven directions from *Smiltene*. It is a roadworkers's capital, the headquarters of the stock company *8.CBR*, which builds roads, bridges, etc. in Vidzeme. A hospital was built in *Smiltene* in 1903 and it is still going strong today.

The owners of the *Smiltene* manor built a manor ensemble with household buildings, greenhouses, creameries and other buildings in the 18th and 19th centuries. Noble House (second half of the 18th century) is a rare architectural monument to wooden buildings. Formation of the manor parks was started along with the construction of the buildings. A monument, called *Split Family* by sculptor Indulis Ranka to victims of the Soviet genocide is found in the centre of the town.

Valdemārpils

A stone memorial to Krišjānis Valdemārs and the Lutheran church in *Valdemārpils*, which is located 130 km from Rīga and 15 km from *Talsi*. 94.8 % of the 1379 inhabitants are Latvian

A town in Kurzeme on the banks of Lake *Sasmaka* - *Valdemārpils* (formerly *Sasmaka*) was first mentioned in historic records from 1582. There is an ancient castle hill in *Valdemārpils*. A hamlet of artisans and merchants was established on the land of *Sasmaka* estate in the beginning of the 17th century. Fishing settlements formed on the banks of Lake *Sasmaka*. *Sasmaka* was given the rights of a city in 1917. It was renamed to *Valdemārpils* in 1926, in the honour of Krišjānis Valdemārs, a prominent Latvian public figure, writer and the founder of the first naval academy in Latvia who lived here between 1835 and 1845. A stone memorial by sculptor D. Jansone in the honour of the eminent townsman was unveiled in 1993.

Wooden buildings from the 18th century are preserved in the eastern part of the city. Its historical centre is a monument to city planning. The *Valdemārpils* Lutheran church (1646) preserves an altarpiece of the Blessed sacrament (17th century), a painted wooden chancel and altar with woodcarvings, which are recognised as a unique and an excellent example of woodcarving art in Kurzeme from the period of late Renaissance and early Baroque. A rural type of a synagogue with a classic two-level roof is also preserved in *Valdemārpils*, however, it is used for other purposes now. 84% of the population in *Valdemārpils* were Jewish at the beginning of the 19th century.

An ancient sacred tree called the *Elku* ("deity") linden (circumference – 8 m, height – 22 m) grows in front of the *Sasmaka* castle. It is the largest and most remarkable *dižliepa* ("great linden") in Latvia, and is regarded as a twin tree. The approximate age of the sacred tree is 350 years. Trees and shrubs of more than 29 different species are found in the 1.8 hectares of the castle park located between the castle and Lake *Sasmaka*.

Livs

The *Mazirbe* Church after a service

Livs, also known as Livonians, are a Finno-Ugric people, who have lived for many centuries in Kurzeme and Vidzeme. The Livs are related to the Finnish tribes, which lived around the Baltic Sea and in what is now Latvia some 3300 years BC. The Liv language evolved around 1 thousand BC. Archaeologists consider that a distinctive Liv culture emerged around the 10th century. The first written record about Livs and their language, which has survived to this day is a report by a monk from Kiev called Sylvester (1056 – 1160), who wrote a chronicle in the 11th century in which he used the ethnic designation *libj*. The first information about Livs in Latvian historical sources is found in the Chronicles of Indriķis. The Vidzeme Livs were the first tribe in Latvia to fall victim to the German Crusaders, and they were drafted to fight against Estonians, Latgallians and other ethnic groups.

Livs suffered great losses during the feudal wars of the 16th to 18th centuries, as well as in the Black Plague epidemic, which struck Latvia in 1710 and 1711. The Liv language disappeared from Rīga and its surroundings in the 16th century and from Vidzeme in the 19th century. The number of Livs in Kurzeme in 1915 was around 3000, but World War I was fatal for the community. In 1915, the German army occupied the coast, and the people were given 24 hours to move out of their villages and at least 10-km inland. Many went into exile. There were only some 1000 Livs left after World War I.

The period of Liv national awakening started between 1920 and 1930, the Liv Association was founded, the Liv Nation Building was built in *Mazirbe*, and two Lutheran congregations were formed in *Kolka* and *Irbe*. Many of the few Livs who were alive in Latvia at the start of World War II perished as a result of Soviet activities in 1940. Many utilised small boats and fled to Sweden. During the Cold War the Kurzeme coast was a frontier zone, and access to it was possible only with military permits. The historical source of employment for the Livs was lost. Liv could not even be listed as a nationality in the Soviet passport.

In the 1970s, the Liv intelligentsia began to legalise the Liv culture. The *Liv Association* is now restored. In 1991, a specially protected cultural and historical zone known as the *Liv Shore* was declared by the State. The Liv Cultural Centre opened its doors. Towards the end of 1999, the Latvian Cabinet accepted a long-term targeted programme, *Livs in Latvia*.

Cēsis

View over the *Cēsis* castle from the castle's park

Cēsis is a city in Vidzeme's *Switzerland*, a place with spectacular scenery. The *Sarkanā* (Raiskums) cliffs, popular among tourists, are located up the *Gauja* River valley from *Raiskums* inn, as well as *Vinters* glen on the left side of the *Gauja* River valley with *Vinters* cave (35 m long), *Zvani* cliff and rippling brooks, *Svētavots* creek glen with *Cīrulīši* cave, *Cēsis* Forest Cemetery, where the distinguished sculptor Kārlis Jansons found his final resting place. Royal ladies and maidens expelled from St. Petersburg court lived in the *House of Princesses* (from the 18th century) in *Rīgas iela* 47 during the 19th century.

Many of the city's buildings are objects of national culture heritage: the Livonian Order's castle, St. John's Church, *Rucka* manor with its park, the old and the new *Cēsis* castle ensemble with park. The territory of present day *Cēsis* was inhabited already in 1000 BC. Cēsis district was first mentioned in the Chronicle of Indriķis in the context of events taking place in 1206, when the local people – vendi – adopted the christian faith. The masonry castle of the Brotherhood of Swords was built next to the vendi people's castle, promoting growth of the adjacent city.

Cēsis was given the rights of a city in 1323. The period of Livonian Order state was a time of prosperity for *Cēsis*, when its name was carried far beyond the Livonian state, it was a member of Hanseatic League and enjoyed its time of glory. Count K. Sievert built the new *Cēsis* castle in 1778, which now houses a museum. The highway Rīga – Pskow was built in 1849 with a 6-km long offshoot to *Cēsis* built in 1868. The railway line Rīga – Pskow was open in 1889. *Cēsis* is presently known for the largest and most contemporary printing house in Eastern Europe and the *Cīrulīši* health resort.

Sigulda and the Gauja National Park

Tautasdziesmu parks ("folksong park") on *Dainu* Hill, where sculptures by the sculptor Indulis Ranka are displayed, is a part of a complex with the *Turaida* hill castle, *Turaida* Church (from 1750), which is the oldest monument to building in wood in Vidzeme region, and are all popular tourist attractions. A favourite of both tourists and newly wed couples is the grave of *Turaidas Roze* ("the Rose of *Turaida*") – Maija (1601 – 1620) next to a linden tree, which is still green and alive as the legend about the love and devotion of Maija.

Sigulda is the administrative centre of the *Gauja* National Park, a city in the Vidzeme highlands, known for unique natural beauty. The most spectacular views over the *Gauja* River valley unfold from here. Between the first and eighth centuries AD, this was the site of the best-fortified Liv castle hills - the *Rati* Hill, as well as the *Turaida*, *Satezele*, *Vilkmesta* and *Vieši* castle hills. The German Crusaders took over the territory. The master of the Livonian Order began to build a

castle in *Sigulda* in 1207, while Rīga bishop started his in 1224 in *Turaida*. *Sigulda* Church (now Lutheran) was started in 1225, and it is the oldest building in *Sigulda*. In 1878, the owner of the *Sigulda* manor, O. Kropotkina, built a new castle in Sigulda.

There is a legend attached to every cave in *Sigulda*. Turaidas Roze was stabbed to death in *Gūtmanis* Cave while keeping her virginity safe from Polish soldiers. Gardener Viktors Heils carved Viktors Cave out of the sandstone so that his beloved one, Turaidas Roze, could see his gardens. *Velnala* ("Devils Cave") was a devil's lair, where he returned after harassing the local people. There is a bobsled and luge track (built in 1986), several slalom ski tracks, a cable tram across the *Gauja* River valley and a 121-m long pedestrian bridge across the *Gauja* River in *Sigulda*. Since 1993, *Sigulda* has been the site of an annual summer opera music festival, organised by doctor Dainis Kalns. There are also traditional ballooning festivals in *Sigulda*.

The Most Modern and Safe Bobsled and Luge Track in Europe

Rolands Upatnieks was the initiator of the construction of a bobsled and luge track with artificial ice. According to bobsled specialists throughout the world, it is one of the fastest and safest tracks on the planet. This is a place where not only Latvian sportsmen improve their skills. Many foreign contestants, too, have achieved respectable results here. Many major international bobsled and luge competitions are held in *Sigulda*. H. A. Samaranch, the president of IOC, during his visit to Latvian sports facilities had a high opinion of the bobsled and luge track at *Sigulda*.

If Latvia was not quite the birthplace of bobsled, Latvians have contributed greatly to the development the sport. The first bobsled tracks in *Mežaparks* and *Āgenskalns* were built at the end of the 19th century and the criteria for evaluating competitions of the two-man luge were developed in Rīga.

At the Lake Placid Winter Olympics in 1980, Vera Zozuļa won gold in the luge, while Ingrīda Amantova took bronze. Both competed with Latvian-made luges, which were considered of a very high quality by specialists. Zintis Ekmanis won the first gold in Latvian two-man bobsled history during the Sarajevo Olympics in 1984.

Jānis Ķipurs became the Olympic champion in the two-man bobsled in 1988 and received the bronze in four-man bobsled together with J. Tonis, G. Osis and V. Kozlovs. The four-man bobsled piloted by Sandis Prūsis in the 2000 season reached second place in the world cup rankings.

The Dainu Hill in *Turaida*. Foreground – *Austras Tree* by sculptor Indulis Ranka (1989, in granite, 600x200x200)

Ludza

Ludza is a border-town in Latgale. It was granted the rights of a town in 1777. The city is located in a beautiful landscape, surrounded by four lakes. The largest of them is Lake Ludza. It is one of the oldest cities in Latvia, mentioned in the Chronicles of Kiev and Ipatia in 1177. There were settlements here already in the 5-8th millennium BC. The Livonian Order built a stone castle here (only the castle-ruins have remained until today) in 1399, around which the city grew. Many Russians have settled in Ludza since time immemorial. There was always a large Jewish community in the city. The metal-fabricating industry, flax and meat processing industries and dairy industry were developed in Ludza after World War II. The city was flooded by labour from Russia and the population structure became even more varied. Only 52.9 % of the 11.5 thousand residents in Ludza are ethnic Latvians.

The Ludza castle ruins and the Chapel of St. Tadeus are historical monuments of national significance. Ludza is a typical Catholic town in Latgale. The artworks and architecture of the town is a confirmation to the residents' faith – the New Roman Catholic Church preserves modern Cross Road sculptures by Jānis Bārda, the Statue of Our Lady, the queen of Earth is located near the Chapel of St. Tadeus. The pedagogue and historian of the region, Jezups Soikans was born and worked in Ludza. His son, painter Juris Soikans donated his works to the city after he return from exile and found his eternal peace in the Ludza Cemetery. Roman Catholic, Lutheran, Russian Orthodox, Old Believer and Seventh Day Adventist congregations work in the city. Before World War II, there was a Jewish synagogue in the city as well, but it was used for other purposes during the years of occupation. There are wooden buildings in Ludza, as well. However, they have suffered considerable damage in fires, especially the one in 1938, when buildings in seven streets burned down.

The Basilica of Aglona

The majestic towers of the Basilica of *Aglona*, the Roman Catholic centre of Latvia, rise high above the green hills and the blue lakes of Latgale, inspiring people to spiritual enlightenment. Thousands of individuals and groups of pilgrims from Latvia, Lithuania, Poland, France come here – to Latgale's Mecca – on the 15th of August every year in order to attain purification of soul. Many succeed in doing so, especially during the night from the 14th to the 15th of August when masses of people experience the sufferings of Christ, sing church hymns, pray and discover the meaning of spiritual life by the twinkle of candlelight. Pope John Paul II was here on 9 September 1993 and blessed Latvia and the people of Latvia. Christianity was initially not welcome in Latvia, most Latgallians continued to live in accordance with their mythological beliefs. The noblewoman Eva Justin Shostovicka supported by the Livonian bishop Nikolai Poplavski suggested to the Dominicans of Vilnius the construction of a cloister and a congregation school in *Aglona* in 1697. The suggestion was successful. The first *Aglona* Church was a wooden structure, built in 1699. A cloister was built next to it. The construction was managed by Eva Justin Shostovicka; she presented the church, the cloister and 17 *sādžas* ("villages") containing 90 peasants to the Dominicans. The Dominicans laid foundations of the present masonry church in 1768. The construction work was lead by the prior Remidi Zahorovski himself. The church is built in Italian Baroque style; it has a couple of triplex towers. Baroque is mixed with elements of Classicism on the facade and the interior of the church. There is a smaller degree of sophistication here than in *Pasiena*. The church is 45-m long, 23 m wide and the towers are 56 m high. About 6000 people can fit inside the church. There are 3 doors on the front, one of which leads to the basement of the church. The towers hold 5 church bells. The Basilica of *Aglona* has one of the oldest organs in Latvia. The organ has been repaired and upgraded several times. There are 10 altars and icons in the church. There are many legends about the icon of *Aglona's* Notre Dame; it is painted by an unknown artist on oak in the 17th century. It is older than the church itself.

Latgale – a Unique Latvia's Region of Ethnography and Culture
Rēzekne

Wooden buildings with rich woodcarvings are typical of towns and cities in Latgale. This building was restored by students from the *Rēzekne* Art College

Latgale's Māra – Latgale's Freedom Monument (to the right), by the sculptors Kārlis and Andrejs Jansons. It was destroyed and rebuilt on several occasions. It is located in Rēzekne facing the Catholic Cathedral of Grieving Mary (to the left)

The inhabitants consider *Rēzekne* the capital of Latgale as the fourth President of Latvia, Kārlis Ulmanis called it in his time. It is located in the centre of the Latgale region at the *Rēzekne* River on the banks of Lake *Rēzekne* (*Kovši*) spread over seven hills. The city gained the rights of a city in 1773.

There was a Latgallian castle in the area between the 10th and the 11th century. The Livonian order built a masonry castle here in 1285 after the German invasion. Eventually settlements appeared in the vicinity of the castle. The composition of the inhabitants changed with the centuries, especially around the turn of the 17th and the 18th century, when *Rēzekne* was flooded by settlers of Russian Old Believer origin. The Russian emper-

or Nicholas I paid a visit to the city in 1846. The first public school was founded in 1826, and in 1831 the first district school was opened. The *Ēglu* pharmacy was open in 1836 and is one of the oldest in Latgale.

Rēzekne is an important transport centre. State highways and international highways Rīga – Moscow, Kauņas – *Daugavpils* – St. Petersburg pass through the city, as well as the railway lines Rīga – Moscow and St. Petersburg – Warsaw.

Several food-processing industries are located in *Rēzekne*. The building material industry is developing rapidly. There is a university, a regional hospital and collages of art and music in the city.

The Curves of the Daugava. Slutišķi

An ethnographic *sādža* in *Daugavpils* district, *Naujene* parish, which covers an area of 129 km², with 6500 inhabitants.

Life in the *Daugavpils* region has always been connected with the largest river in Latvia, the *Daugava* River. The local inhabitants are mainly employed with fishing, livestock breeding and agriculture. A Decree by the Russian Tsar stated that the arrangement of settlements should be along roads. The trend is still visible, however, most *sādžas* next to roads are dominated by Russian inhabitants. Latgallians were always more rebellious in spirit and usually formed their settlements near spectacular sites, along rivers or lakes, on hillsides, in forest meadows, despite the Decree.

The *Daugava* River valley is no exception. A nature reserve, *Daugavas Loki*, was established to preserve the unique landscape, cultural and historical heritage of the valley. The reserve covers a total area of 10.5 thousand hectares. Established scenic lookouts provide views over the spectacular landscape. The deserve is suited for srecreation and tourism. A plan for development of the *Daugava* River valley was drafted, agreements are concluded with local authorities on specific plans of action; people from the local communities are engaged.

Naujene is the most unique part of the *Daugava* River valley with the greatest natural diversity. It is located 19 km from *Daugavpils*. *Naujene* was first mentioned in historical documents from 1275, when crusaders of Livonian Order destroyed the old *Naujene* castle and started the construction of a stone castle. A model of the *Dinaburg* castle can now be observed in the ruins of the original. There are more than 10 different archaeological and cultural monuments in *Naujene* today, the Roman Catholic churches of *Sprukti* (1933) and *Juzefova* (1936 – 1961), the *Juzefova* park from the 18th century, Marhova discovery track and the spirit distillery are some of the objects. The major roads are *Daugavpils* – Vitebska and *Daugavpils* – St. Petersburg. *Latgales AVIO* airport is operational in the parish as well, with flights *Daugavpils* – *Liepāja* – Copenhagen.

Crucifixes in Latgale

Crucifixes in *Līksna*, *Daugavpils* district and *Aknīste*, *Jēkabpils* district

The suffering of Christ carved in wood – crucifixes, are common in Latgale's rural areas. Crucifixes have grown into one with the essence of the Latgallian deeply religious spirit. Latgallians call them *kristi* ("Christs"). *Kristi* are designed to make people lift their eyes. A Latgallian would do so, stop a while, take of his hat and say a prayer. Crucifixes gather and unite people. Since churches were rather far apart, a tradition of holding Catholic services in May at crosses of local villages – *sādžas* – was introduced in the late-19th century. A person of choice held them without a priest. The selected person was usually a woman with a loud voice and the qualities of a good organiser. There were some 2000 crosses at the end of the 19th century. Initially it was considered that setting up the crosses was something only Jesuits did (the late-17th century) in Latgale. Jesuits, though foreigners, learned the Latgallian dialect and taught Latgallians to write and read. Jesuits carved the holy crosses and placed them together with altarpieces in Latgallian sacred sites. This was the beginning of outdoor crucifix tradition.

Kristi were often shaped in complete ignorance of body proportions. Professional artists could not be involved, therefore local artists, usually monastic artisans, had to do the carving. The greatest emphasis was usually put on head with the crown, while legs and the middle body were often disproportional. It is probably just the simplicity that made Latgallians accept and preserve the sculptures until this very day. The most distinguished wood sculptors, who made *kristi*, are Jānis Cibuļskis, Jānis Kļavinskis, Pēteris Kozuļkaža, grandfather Bogdans, Kazimirs Ruskulis, Antons Gleizds, Antons Kivkucāns, and Antons Removičs.

The Rundāle Castle

The *Rundāle* castle is the most significant monument to Baroque and Rococo architecture in Latvia. The cornerstone for the castle was laid by the Duke of Kurzeme, Ernst Biron, in 1736. The architect for the castle was Francesco Bartalomeo Rastrelli, but the artists came from St. Petersburg. More than one and a half thousand people were employed in its construction. After 1740, when the death of Anna Ivanovna put a halt to the exalted career of the castle's owner, E. J. Biron was arrested and sent into exile. Biron was pardoned in 1763. He returned to Kurzeme with architect Rastrelli. The *Rundāle* castle was finished in 1768. Italian painters Francesco Martini and Carlo Cuki, as well as a master of decorative work from Berlin, Johann Mikhail Graf, were invited to do interior design. The stir of court life settled after the death of the old duke (in 1772), because Duke Peter Biron rarely stayed at the castle. Royalty gathered at the castle once again during the time of Count Platon Zubov, but during the war in 1812, it was plundered. It was renovated in 1822. During the period of ownership by the family of Count Shuvalov (1822 – 1920), the castle was quiet again. World War I brought new destruction to the castle. The work of reconstruction, started in 1933, was put an end to by World War II. A granary was installed in the castle in 1940, and wet grain was stored directly on parquet. It was not until 1972, that a new restoration of the Rundāle castle was begun. A museum was established.

The castle ensemble covers a land of more than 60 hectares. There are 138 rooms in two floors. The galleries and the two main stairwells on the first floor, as well as the Small Gallery are the only preserved examples of Rastrelli's early style. The most ornate rooms are the Ballroom, now known as the White Room, remarkable with its white stucco relief work and the uplifting mood, the Rose Room and the Gold Room, the former Throne Room. The distinguished Latvian artist and cultural worker Imants Lancmanis has been of key significance in the restoration of the Rundāle castle.

The Cesvaine Castle

An architect from Berlin, Hans Griesenbach, designed the *Cesvaine* castle in 1896. H. Griesenbach was an independent construction manager since 1876, and had his own practice in the 1880's. The *Cesvaine* castle was built by H. Griesenbach and August George Dinklage. The two have built several castles in Germany as well.

The *Cesvaine* castle was built as a hunting castle with ornate decorations harmonised with the surrounding environment. Its architectural style is a form of eclectic romanticism with medieval, Romantic and Gothic elements.

The combination of styles creates an impression of ancient architecture. The U-shaped building has an entrance in the middle section with a ramp to drive up to the monumental portal. The outer layer of the walls is composed of split and treated granite stones. Russian artisans from Latgale did this work. No explosives were used to split the stones. The stones were first examined for cracks with a small hammer, and then split with a large

hammer along the natural cracks that were found. The steep roof was built in Gothic style. The mannered outline of the terminal pediment on the building's left wing is topped with a heraldic statue of a wolf, because there are images of a fox, a wolf and a lion on the coat of arms of baron Wulf, the owner of the castle. There is a wolf image in the coat of arms of *Gulbene's* baron Wolf, as well. The only difference is in the wolves' tails – Wulf's wolf has its tail pointing up, while Wolf's wolf has his tail down. Baron Wulf despised baron Wolf, and people say that the iron wolf statue was placed on the roof with its tail turned towards *Gulbene* because of his dislike.

The castle is well preserved. The manifold interior is decorated with beautiful wooden staircase, which has handrails carved in Renaissance style. There are ceiling paintings with plants and animals, a portrait of Diana, and Renaissance style fireplace in the Hunters Room (Tower section). The *Cesvaine* castle has housed a high school since 1919.

The *Šlokenbekas* manor-castle is located in *Milzkalne*, *Tukums* district. It was first mentioned in 1484 as a fort of the Livonian Order. Reconstruction work on the manor was started in 1977. The rectangular complex of buildings is surrounded by buildings on three sides and a fortification wall with loopholes on the west side. Both gate towers with gambrel (the mid-18th century) and residential buildings (1841) are preserved

Latvia's Manor Architecture

There is at least one manor, included on the list of historical and cultural monuments of the Republic of Latvia, in every district of Latvia. There are several in *Talsi* district, and one of them is the *Nogales* manor with a residential building (1880) and a park in *Vandzene* village. It was owned by baron Fircks and served as a hunting castle, built in neo-Renaissance style. The ceiling decorations, fireplaces and stoves are preserved.

A manor was a nobleman's homestead. The manor land was considerable and a common feature of a manor in Latvia starting with the 16th century – in 1920 some 48 % of Latvia's territory was made up of land belonging to manors. A nobleman was the representative of the state with judicial powers within the territory of his manor. The residential buildings, which are not fortified castles, are considered manors or noblemen's homesteads. They appeared in Latvia in the 17th century as copies of West European noblemen's rural farms. The manors built during this period still have some fortifications: they are quadrangular formations with the residential buildings and household buildings around an inner yard, connected by sections of walls with loopholes (e.g. the *Šlokenbeka* manor).

The architecture of manors was dominated by the Baroque style in the 18th century. Protrusions were added to the edges of rectangular buildings and the small details are typical of the Baroque style (metalwork on doors, gable windows). The manor architecture flourished starting from 1750 and reached its culmination in 1800 (Classicism). Many manors were designed by K. Haberland, Guarengi from Italy, Berlics from Switzerland, as well as architects from Rīga, V. Bokslaf and others.

The organic development of architectural styles came to a halt in Latvia and West Europe around 1850, and it was replaced by eclectic forms, composed of architectural styles from different periods in time, and ignored the essence and idea behind these styles. Gothic elements were especially popular in manor architecture: ornate groupings of buildings in Romantic style, topped with jagged pediments and towers with tablings. The manor buildings were handed over to local authorities and public organisations after the proclamation of Latvian State in 1918. They served as schools and recreation facilities.

The *Jaunmokas* Palace in *Tukums* district.

Kazdanga

The *Kazdanga* palace (*Liepāja* district) and a three-section bridge across glen

Kazdanga is known for its beautiful landscape, cultural and historical heritage.

In 1520, Bishop Martin Levin turned the *Kazdanga* manor-house over to Carl Manteifel, who was previously in the bishop's service. The family Manteufel lived in the manor-house for 14 generations during the next 300 years. Legends tell that the family started with bishop's misbegotten son. The Bishop of Kurzeme happened to seduce a servant in Piltene – a Latvian girl who became pregnant. He made his dog keeper marry the girl. The man was later rewarded with the title of baron.

Construction of the *Kazdanga* palace began in 1800 in the time of Carl G. E. Manteufel. Its architect was George Johan Berlics from Berlin. The local peasants were involved in the construction. The Corinthian pillars along the garden's facade are handcrafted by the local residents. The palace is built in the Classical style. The palace was greatly damaged during World War I. It was restored in 1925 – 1927. The stone bridge (the *Vaidu* Bridge) was built across the glen in 1840.

The largest dendrology park in Latvia is located in *Kazdanga*. It covers an area of 173 hectares, houses about 300 species of trees and bushes (127 foreign species) and was started around the turn of the 18th and 19th centuries. Many sites with open view are created in the park. There are about 20 ponds and many granite benches. A sandstone vase (from 1850) with Demetra, the ancient Greek goddess, is found in a sculptural open-air exposition. The vase was dedicated to a method of land reclamation using closed drainage, which was applied in *Kazdanga* for the first time in the Russian Empire. The first ponds in Latvia were built here in 1873. Several schools of agriculture were open, too. The students of the schools – girls and boys – were not allowed to swim in the same pond and thus the ponds were named the Girls' pond and the Boys' pond respectively. The *Kazdanga* palace now houses the *Kazdanga* School of Agriculture.

The Ungurmuiža Manor

The name of the *Ungurmuiža* Manor comes from its first owner, Ungern. Lieutenant-general Baltasar von Kampenhausen purchased the estate in 1728. He started to rebuild the old household buildings and to build a new residential building. The residential building was finished in 1751 – 1752. The estate is built in the Baroque style. The single-storied building has mansard roof. The central section of it is accented by the roof construction. The facade is decorated with flat pilasters, window cases, roof ledges, corner ware, and ironwork. There are wall paintings and tile stoves in the *Ungurmuiža* Manor from the 18th century. A teahouse, a superintendent's house, a granary and household buildings, and a park are all part of the manor's ensemble.

An important role in education during the 18th century in Vidzeme was played by the Herrnhuter brotherhood congregations. Some noblemen in Vidzeme supported them, the owner of the *Ungurmuiža* Manor, Kampenhausen did so especially. It is possible that he was introduced to their ideas as early as in 1721 while in Germany, assigned on a mission by the Russian tsar. When the first Herrnhuter envoys, brother Christian Davis and brother Timothy Fihdler, arrived in Vidzeme in the autumn of 1729, the owner of the *Ungurmuiža* Manor,

Architectural monument – the *Ungurmuiža* Manor in *Cēsis* district

Kampenhausen, visited them and offered his support. A Herrnhuter brother worked as a teacher in the *Ungurmuiža* Manor in 1737, and soon learned Latvian as did all of the Herrnhuter. Ill-minded noblemen, who did not like the work of the Herrnhuter, gained the support of Russian tsarina Elisabeth, and the brotherhood was outlawed in 1742. The tsarina's decision was softened thanks to B. Kampenhausen's courage, persistence and influence on her.

A Latvian Rural Homestead

Groups of ethnically authentic rural homesteads in the *Vecpiebalga* district, Vidzeme region

Storks, including the black storks, which are very rare in other European countries, often nest near rural homesteads

The village is the oldest form of settlement in the territory of Latvia. It was gradually replaced by single family homesteads. The process occurred more quickly in Vidzeme, Kurzeme and Zemgale. Villages remained along the coastal areas, where people engaged in fishing. In the Eastern Latvian region of Latgale, farmers' homesteads continued to be associated with specific villages – *solas* – for a longer period of time. The average Latvian family homestead had several buildings – a residential building, a livestock shed, a threshing barn, a granary and a bathing house or sauna, known as the pirts and an outhouse. In poorer homesteads, a single building could fulfil several functions – that of a livestock shed, a barn, a granary, etc. The residential building was usually placed in the centre of the homestead – at the highest and driest location. The other buildings were usually arranged around the courtyard of the residential building, while the pirts and the outhouse were located at a distance.

The arrangement of buildings in Vidzeme and Kurzeme tend to be rather scattered around a courtyard, but they were joined together with hedges between them. In Latgale, the courtyards were rectangular with buildings around it joined with a high hedge. Every Latvian homestead had a fruit orchard. One could make judgments about the wealth of a farmer by looking at the size of his homestead and the arrangement of the buildings. The size of the family and livestock, amount of crop and other goods produced and stored in the farm were taken into consideration when planning buildings.

Homesteads in various regions were unique in different ways, but everywhere in Latvia, farmers took pride in maintaining order and cleanliness within the territory that was surrounded by the farm's trees. Latvian women were justifiably proud of their beautiful flower gardens, and courtyards were always carefully swept. On festive occasions, Latvians decorated the whole of the homestead with birch-boughs and with various items of folk art. To a Latvian, the homestead is a source of strength for the respective family and dynasty.

Northern Lights

Northern Lights in Latvia's night sky (2000)

The phenomenon of northern lights or *aurora borealis* is usually visible in a circular pattern around the magnetic poles of the Earth beyond the polar circles, but sometimes it is visible even in Latvia. Latvians use to say then – *kāvi* in the sky. The sight is impressive and it may last only a few minutes or the whole night. Northern lights lasted several hours in some parts of Latvia in the winter of 2000. Different figures and crosses appear, change brightness and scenes in the sky rather quickly. *Kāvi* flowed in Latvia's sky in the end of 1980's and the beginning of 1990's on several occasions. Pink, green and yellow fluvial patches were visible in the sky. On 27 January 1992, the bright red and blue rays subdued the light from stars entirely.
The northern lights are visible in Latvia at the maximum peak of solar activity.

The Ethnographic Open-air Museum of Latvia – Europe's Largest

Fisherman's homestead, a captain's house in Ethnographic Open-air Museum in Rīga, on the banks of Lake *Jugla*

The museum was founded in 1924 and is one of the oldest and richest in Europe. The first exposition – *Rizgu* threshing barn – was exhibited in 1928. In 1932, the year of opening, there were 6 expositions in the museum – 5 from Vidzeme, 1 from Latgale. Latvian homesteads from Vidzeme, Zemgale, Latgale and Kurzeme as well as several public buildings (*Usmas* Church, *Bornes* Church, *Mežuļi* Brothers' congregation house, etc.) were exhibited in the museum before World War I.

Ethnographic Open-air museum of Latvia was established by donations from the State, public organisations and individual benefactors. Several ensembles of regionally characteristic buildings (a Latgale *sādža* from the 19th century, a Kurzeme Liv peasant – fisherman homestead, etc.) were arranged during the years after the war. Tools from homesteads of peasants, fishermen and craftsmen were collected and preserved. There is an inn, windmill, blacksmith forge, and a number of churches (services are still held in the *Usmas* Church today). The museum hosts many exhibitions and cultural events. On the first weekend of June, exhibitions and markets of folk arts take place every year in the Ethnographic Open-air Museum. Masters of fourteen different crafts work in the museum: including blacksmiths, spoon-carvers, weavers, potters, and beekeepers. Folklore festivals in celebration of various holidays in folk-tradition manner – Christmas, Easter, *Līgo*, *Miķeļdiena* – take place in the museum. There are also art exhibitions on display in the Ethnographic Open-air museum of Latvia.

Pape. The Seashore of Kurzeme Preserves Ancient Traditions and Customary Fishermen Lifestyle

Papes Koņu village in Kurzeme

Papes village is located in the southern-most corner of Kurzeme next to the Baltic Sea. This district is distinguished by great national material and spiritual values – ancient traditions, folk costumes, as well as ancient rural architectural monuments. *Pape* was formed when three fishing villages grew together – *Priedniekgals*, *Papes* village and *Papes Koņi*. The combined length of the village is 8 km. It is located in *Rucava* parish between Lake *Pape* and the sea.

The settlements in *Papes Koņi* and *Priedniekgals* are from the second half of the 19th century and the 20th century. The settlements are scattered and arranged around single or double courtyards. Not only the functions of a threshing barn, but also those of a livestock barn and stables were often shared under the same roof of a fishing homestead.

Several homesteads are in the *Papes Koņi* protected zone. A granary at *Mikjāņi* homestead has a rare system of ventilation. There are buildings in the village where reeds are used for heat insulation in order to protect the logs from rotting. A livestock barn in *Papes Koņi* has

walls covered with bundles of reeds. Residential buildings, livestock barns, threshing barns in Kurzeme were built on unique sets of foundations, effective in protecting the logs from getting soaked and rotting. This practice evolved around the middle of the 18th century. These kind of foundations was especially useful to livestock barns. However, the traditional way of construction was widely use in *Pape* as well as late as in the 19th century. Oak, fir or pine logs were placed directly on higher grounds. Another method seen in the remains of granary building of *Jūrnieki* homestead is where the corners of a log structure rest upon vertically dug-in oak or fir logs. The most popular roofing during the 19th century and the beginning of the 20th century was reeds. Landless peasants and ones with a little land earned their living by scything and binding reeds to be used for roofing buildings in the vicinity of Lake *Pape*. Reed roofs are still preserved in *Pape*. There is a lighthouse (built in 1890) on a 4 – 5 m high dune at some distance from the sea.

Latvians have always taken good care and loved their horses, their best helper in all kinds of farm work. The good qualities of the horse – *kumeliņš* (colt) – like beauty and importance in a farmer's life are sung about in numerous folksongs. The Latvian breed of horses was officially recognised in 1952. It was created by improving the local breed with Hanover, Oldenburg, Trakehner breeds from Germany, as well as Arabian and purebred English breeds. The breed has versatile uses – the horses are suitable for sports, show jumping, show-riding and tourist entertainment. The horses may be hitched to wagons and used for different farming functions.

There are four major horse-breeding facilities in Latvia: the *Tērvete* stud-farm in *Dobele* district, the *Burtnieki* stud-farm in *Valmiera* district, the *Turība* stud-farm in *Preiļi* district, and the *Okte* stud-farm in *Talsi* district, as well as some 29 other privately owned stud-farms which specialise in one breed only. There are some 19 200 horses in Latvia. Horses are bred and trained for sports and later exported to Germany, Denmark, Sweden, Netherlands, Italy, Estonia, Poland and Russia. Breeding stallions are brought to Latvia from Germany, Denmark and Sweden.

Show-jumping competitions take place every year February through October. Latvian sportsmen have successfully participated in international competitions, as well. Wagon hauling competitions took place in Latvia until 1989, where the horses' durability and strength were tested. There are recreational riding facilities in *Līgatne* (*Cēsis* district), *Turaida* (*Rīga* district) and elsewhere. Horses are also used for medical purposes in Latvia. Specialists use horseback riding therapies at the rehabilitation centre *Vaivari* in *Jūrmala* city, the sanatorium *Līgatne* in *Cēsis* district and the *Kleisti* facility in *Rīga* district.

Pedvāle – JUNESCO's Culture Project

The *Pedvāle* Open-air Museum of Art in the *Abava* River valley was started by its director and sculptor, Ojārs Feldbergs. He is also a member in the Council of the *Abava* River Valley, a cultural and historical area of special protection. The *Abava* River valley is listed in World Monument Watch 100 Most Endangered Sites. Not long ago, the *Abava* River valley was protected only by a complex reserve. It is starting to gain increasingly more significance in Latvia's cultural life. The *Pedvāle* manor was abandoned, but is now being restored, both the buildings and the surrounding area. The glen was overgrown. Its true magnificence was rediscovered after it was cleared from shrub and the noble oak trees, great linden trees and beech trees stood out. The landscape is being reconstructed to as it might have been during the time of its owner, baron Volfgang von Fircks. The baron's descendants consider that the *Pedvāle* manor was the best treated of the family Fircks' former properties. The locals claim to have sometimes caught a glimpse of the beautiful Fircks' daughter at midday by the creek. Her grave is on a hillock by the glen.

The *Templa* (Temple) Hill is also brought to its earlier order. It provides beautiful views over the *Abava* River valley.

The old orchard at the manor is being brought to life again, where the artist's creations have found their place. Art exhibitions and events are organised in the *Pedvāle* Open-air Museum of Art increasingly often. A wide range of artists with local reputation and international fame, as well as students of the Academy of Art take part in the exhibitions. The art objects are homogenous to the surrounding environment. Some works are usually displayed indoors, as well.

The sculptor Ojārs Feldbergs continues to develop the *Pedvāle* Open-air Museum of Art. Every year brings new, untraditional art exhibitions with many participants, observers and critics.

The Āraiši Lake Castle

The baron of *Cēsis*, Karl Sievers was informed about the fact that there was an ancient architectural monument on an island in Lake *Āraiši* as early as 1876. He conducted the first archaeological excavations at the site.

Three quarters of the 2500 square m occupied by the castle were investigated during ten seasons of excavation in 1965 – 1969 and 1975 – 1979. First, the water level of the lake had to be lowered by about one meter. Dams were built around excavation sites using archaeological stratum, and water was pumped away with motor pumps. A Latgallian island castle was found, which was inhabited in the 9th and 10th centuries. There was a complex of residential and household buildings well protected by a fortification system. The *Āraiši* castle had been burned by enemy armies and never renewed. The water level was then about 1.5 m lower than it is today. Remains of wooden buildings and artifacts made of organic materials were well preserved in the water.

The government took a decision to reconstruct the *Āraiši* Lake castle in 1983. The project was worked out by archaeologist Jānis Apals and architect Dzintars Driba. The lower parts of the buildings were restored as copies of the originals. The missing upper parts were reconstructed using fragments found on the site, which were assembled together in a logic structure by taking into account ethnographic features. Copies of ancient tools found at the site – narrow-blade axes, gouges, grid-stones and clubs were used in reconstruction after 1990. The *Āraiši* Lake castle is a unique archaeological open-air museum, which gives an inside view of ancient Latgallian lifestyle during the Viking era. Different events (like honey festivals, etc.) with the participation of folklore groups, are held in the lake castle during summer.

Hill Castles – Latvia's Cultural History Dates back to about 10 000 Years

Asote hill castle near *Jēkabpils*. A legend tells that there was once a Latvian castle on the hill. It had a very distinct shape of a hill castle until World War I, but it was deformed by a fortification with underground tunnels

Latvian hill castles were first mentioned in historical documents from 853, when the Swedish Vikings lead by Olaf plundered Kurish lands, pillaged the *Jūrpils* (*Grobiņu*) castle and attacked *Apūle*.

Hill castles (or hill forts) are ancient fortified settlements built on high hillocks, peninsulas, sometimes on lake or swamp islands. Hill castles usually had steep sides, a flat and even top, fortification walls and moats, terraces on hillsides. Only some of the 470 known Latvian hill castles sites are fully investigated. Hill castles with high fortification walls around the flat tops are more common in Kurzeme and Zemgale. Hill castles with low fortification walls and small moats, as well as hill castles with terraces are characteristic to Latgale. Hill castles without walls and terraces are considered to be older, although some of them were still inhabited in the 12th and 13th centuries (for example, *Priekuļu Sāruma* Hill).

Most of the hill castles mentioned in historical documents from the 13th century (*Jersika, Mežotne, Tērvete*, and others) had high fortification walls on the level side. Even the *Doles Klaņģi* hill castle is of this type, though it was built in the end of Bronze Age and was abandoned during first decades AD. Judging from the size and location of the castles, their chief purpose was to protect tribal lands and regions against foreign invasion and local warfare. Some hill castles were located near the main routes of transport, some – in the centre of a region or lands. Castles were located in districts with sparse population to protect wealthier lands from foreign invasion. The defence capacity of hill castles was considerable and battles around them were fierce, some are described in the Chronicle of *Indriķis* and the Chronicle of *Atskaņu*. Towns sprang up around the castles. They may be considered the beginning of present day cities of *Rīga, Kandava, Sabile, Bauska, Cēsis, Ludza* and others.

Spring

Spring starts when the snow begins to melt and the rivers break the ice and carry it away. Usually it happens in the end of March or the beginning of April. Spring lasts about two months. If snow melts fast, it may cause floods and great damage, especially within the river basins of the *Daugava* and *Lielupe* rivers. Frosts are common in early spring, causing damage to the blooming orchards and seedlings. The temperature stays above +5°C only at the end of April.

The weather becomes dry in May due to continental currents and 9-12 days of the month are perfectly clear. The land has to be prepared and seeded early, while it is still moist. Spring is one of the most beautiful seasons in Latvia, described by Latvian writer, Jānis Jaunsudrabiņš: *Where else would you find spring like this, where birch trees glow in rose-colored light, a whole grove of young trees. There is nothing in the world like the aroma when they bud and when they bloom! Where else does the ice sound like it does in Latvia's rivers while rushing off to the sea ... Remember the time of blossoms, how it approaches. First with the humble, white anemones, then the blue palazdītes on the hazel hill, next the bright streams of March marigolds till all the creeks and meadows are filled with countless flowers.* The migrating birds return from the southern lands – glittering flocks of cranes, geese and swans glide along the blue sky in gay chatter. Storks, thrushes and swallows also return. Nightingales engage in enthusiastic singing in the bird-cherry trees.

Latvia's Swamps Preserve Bird and Animal Species, which Have Become Very Rare in the Rest of the World

Swamps cover 10 % of Latvia's territory and total some 6400 square km. The largest swamps are located in the coastal lowlands and in the plains in Eastern Latvia. Swamps started to form as early as the end of the Ice Age. All swamps form either when vegetation overgrows lakes or when plains become marshy due to lack of drainage. The processes are still continuing today.

A distinction is made between highland (or moss) swamps, lowland (or grassland) swamps and other swamps. The largest highland swamps in Latvia are the *Teiči* swamp (in the *Madona* and *Jēkabpils* districts), the *Cena* moor land (Rīga district), and the *Ķemeri-Smārde* moor land (Rīga district). The largest lowland swamps are the *Seda* swamp in *Valka* district, *Peikstuļnīca-Sala* swamp in *Ludza* district. A typical example to intermediate swamps is *Zodēni* swamp in *Balvi* district. Many swamps are protected by law; many are national parks or reserves. *Teiči* swamp has been a reserve since 1982.

Peat is extracted from swamps in Latvia. It is the major fuel mineral found in Latvia. Its significance is bound to increase as the resources of other fossil fuels are used up. Latvia's peat reserves are equal to 1.2 billion tons of coal. In addition peat is a renewable resource – a 1-m thick layer builds up in 1000 years, which gives 6 million cubic m every year. Peat is mostly used for heating and livestock bedding. There is a continuous increase in the amount of peat extracted from year to year. Well-decomposed ooze is used in medicine. It is common in many Latvia's swamps, especially in *Sloka* (*Ķemeri* spa), *Pladi*, *Ķūdrājs* (Peat-land) *Nr.5* near *Daugavpils*.

Several swamps in Latvia are included in reserve territories like the *Slītere* National Park (*Bažu* swamp), *Gauja* National Park (*Suda* swamp), and the *Teiči* reserve–swamp. There are also cranberry and botanical reserves. *Teiči* swamp is the largest one, where a primeval ecosystem is preserved. Some 12-15 flowering plant species are found in every swamp, mostly moss related. Swamps with pine trees have characteristically well developed shrub stands, swamp marsh tea, heather, blueberry, red bilberry, delicious cloudberry, but mostly – cranberry.

The lowland swamps are dominated by dwarf birch and black alder. There are 14 species of lichen, 9 fern species, 37 moss species, and 141 species of seeding plants. 8 species are included in *Latvia's Sarkanā Grāmata* (Red Book) of protected species. Wild boar, elk, deer, and hare live in swamps, too. Wolves, racoons, martens, and badgers are common in swamps. Beaver, mink and otter live in the water. The Grey crane is a rare and protected swamp bird in Latvia. It was a common bird in the beginning of the 20th century, however, due to land reclamation and reproduction problems the population has decreased. Crane calls still echo over Latvia's swamps, especially in the *Teiči* swamp. A patient wild life watcher may observe the beautiful and graceful crane dances, guided by an invisible conductor.

The swamp is also the habitat of the relatively rare short-eared owl. They choose open areas, shrubby meadows, and are sometimes active in daytime, as well. The Black stork is also a protected bird, listed in the *Sarkanā Grāmata*. It prefers woodlands, swamps and places near water for nesting.

Summer

The Latvian summer lasts from June until September. June is often rather chilly, the average temperature is +13-15°C. Sowing and planting of potatoes and vegetables is finished by the beginning of June. July and August are the warmest months of summer. The average temperature in July is +16°C in *Liepāja*, +18°C in *Rīga*, +18°C in *Rēzekne*. Although the difference in temperature between Kurzeme and Latgale is not as great as it is in winter, it is still colder in Kurzeme. There are 12-18 rainy days per month in summer. The end of summer is usually less cloudy as the continental winds carry in warm and dry air from southern grasslands of Russia. There are 20 – 30 sunny days in July and August, when water warms up in lakes, rivers and the sea and people go to beaches along the Gulf of Rīga. This is the most responsible and busy time of year to people in the countryside, the only chance to harvest everything the earth supplies. The middle of summer – the 23rd of June, is the largest and most beautiful of Latvian celebrations. All the hills in Latvia flare with bonfires, *Līgo* songs echo over the land on *Līgo* night. This is the culmination of summer, everything blossoms and a heady aroma fills the air. Next comes linden blossom and there is hardly any place in Latvia, where the aroma does not reach. The nights are short, warm and light. They are especially enjoyable in the country; mist rises from valleys and creeks, corncrakes call over ripening fields of rye as the night approaches, but it never gets dark. Sometimes thunderstorms and hail bring damage to the fields of grain in July and August. The first frosts come at the end of August, and nights become colder. The sky is clear and starlit in at this time of year. Shooting stars are often visible.

Līgo – on 23 June – the Most Beautiful of Latvian National Celebrations

The largest and most beautiful of Latvian celebrations is *Jāņi* on June 23 – the summer solstice. Latvians pick meadow flowers and dress up for the night. Neighbours, relatives and friends with flowers and weeds in their hands and wreaths of flowers and crowns of oak leaves on their heads gather for collective *Jāņi* celebration. On this night both married and single women wear wreaths of flowers in their hair, which is otherwise a practice of single women and girls only. All Latvia's hills are lit up with bonfires and *Līgo* songs echo over the land. Special attention is paid to men called Jānis. People sing songs, drink beer, eat special *Jāņi* cheese, play games and jump bonfire. Young couples go looking for fern flower, which blooms for lovers only in Jani night. The continuous change of seasons in nature ruled the development of Latvian traditions. People generously sacrifice to their ancestors in late autumn during the season of *veļi* (souls of ancients). Christmas is celebrated in solemn peace while honouring God. There is a tradition of stargazing on New Year's Eve, followed by a booming celebration. The *Mārtiņi* festival on November 10 allows Latvians to think back on the joys and difficulties of the past year. All outdoor work is finished before the festival. Next comes the joyous season of *ķekatas* (when people dress up as birds, animals or mythological characters and go from house to house). The Christian traditions are brought together with folk customs. Despite the fact that Latvians have been subjected to various forms of alien rule over the centuries, they have always preserved their holiday traditions and family celebrations, when close and distant relatives meet. The most important festivals for Latvian families traditionally have been Christening (when name is given to a baby), weddings and funerals. The most important elements of the Christening ceremony were the feast, *pādes dīdīšana* (*pāde* is a baby, which has not been given a name yet, and *dīdīšana* is a process when the baby is dandled and danced by uncles and aunts) and the ceremonial hanging of the baby's cradle. Weddings are the most ornate celebrations for families. Krišjānis Barons, when compiling and arranging Latvian folk songs, devoted a special place to wedding songs, bringing together traditions from various regions of Latvia and grouping folk songs that were relevant to the various aspects of courtship and marriage in three volumes. Latvian wedding traditions even today maintain elements from the past – the stealing of the bride, the battle of songs between the relatives for the bride and the relatives for the groom, a process of *mičošana* (where the crown which unmarried women traditionally wear in Latvian folk costumes is removed from the bride, to be replaced with the headscarf that is traditional for married women), dowry inspection, etc. Funeral traditions have to do with the relationship between life and death in Latvia. There are deeply philosophic and harmonized ceremonies, which relate to nature and continuum. Outward desperation and exaggerated sorrow are not the norm in Latvian funerals. The deceased person is spoken of with a good word.

Gauja
River-crossing Facilities

River-crossing facility over the *Gauja* River at *Līgatne*

Brotherhoods of river-men formed as early as the 17th century. The job of the members of these brotherhoods was to transport cargo, people and carriages from one side of the river to the other and on larger rivers - from boats to riverside. The work of river-men, as well as crossing fees, were regulated by articles signed by the governor-general.

River-men signed contracts with merchants and guaranteed the safety of the cargo. The river-crossing facilities were located near important transportation routes and provided coast-to-coast access in places, where there was no bridge.

Rivers were major natural obstacles on the plains and for that reason gravel roads ran along them. The modern road network evolved along the same premises. Fords and river-crossing devices were used to shorten distances. Local road networks in winter often differed from those in summer.

There were especially many river-crossing devices along the larger rivers – the *Daugava*, *Gauja*, *Aiviekste*, and others.

Railway lines supported the highways along the right side of the *Daugava* River. *Krustpils* railway station is a node of railway lines connecting Rīga, *Daugavpils* and *Rēzekne*, as well as five highways, however, there was no bridge over the *Daugava* River here for a long time. Traffic, the transportation of goods and people was organised with the help of a river-crossing device. A bridge was built here in 1936, but it was destroyed in 1941 at the beginning of World War II. The river-crossing device operated once again until 1960, when the bridge between *Krustpils* and *Jēkabpils* was rebuilt.

The trade routs to Poland were serviced by river-crossing device at *Daugavieši*. The one at *Dunava* provided access to the roads on the right side of the *Daugava* River, as did the device on the *Baldone-Birzgale* road. Many river-crossing devices connected both sides of the *Gauja* River only few years ago. The river-crossing device in *Līgatne* is the last one still used.

Livestock Breeding

In the post-war years, Latvia's dairy industry was based on a continual increase in the number of animals. The dairy industry was closely linked to the Latvian Brown breed of cows, known for its good productivity. After the collapse of the Soviet Union, the Latvian dairy industry was aimed towards quality growth. Careful work is being done to improve the livestock feed, introduce new and highly productive varieties of cows, especially in the dairy industry. Latvian dairy exports to the Western Europe are once again on the rise. Sheep, rabbit and pig farming is developing, special goat varieties are bred. Even fallow deer, mouflon sheep and reindeer are now more common in Latvia.

Many beautiful Latvian traditions are connected with the first day of letting the livestock out to pasture in the spring or *rumulēšana*, when cows and horses are crowned with wreaths and crowns of flowers on *Zāļu* ("Greenery") Eve. Many Latvian writers write about their childhood days of being shepherds. Horses, cows, sheep and other farm animals are sung about in many Latvian folksongs.

Milk was first produced in Latvia in the 1st millennium BC. In Latvian folklore and in the eyes of Latvians over the centuries, milk and dairy products have been symbols of prosperity and success. When a job proceeded quickly, it was, the Latvians say, *moving as if through butter*. Dairy products were also sacrificed to the ancient deity Māra, the Mother of the Earth and the Home. Butter was considered to be one of the most valuable stores a household could have. A dictionary from the 17th century lists the following dairy products: sweet milk, sour milk, fermented milk, cream, butter, steamed milk (cottage cheese), and cheese. In the 19th century, Latvia's farmers became increasingly involved in international markets. Farmers from Vidzeme travelled to Paris to participate in world's dairy exhibitions in 1866 and to Vienna to attend similar events in 1872. At the end of the 19th century Latvia was an important territory for dairy farming, and colleagues from Denmark, Germany and Ireland came to study new methods. Co-operative dairy farms started to appear. In the 1930's, dairy farming in Latvia was a most profitable enterprise, and most of the produce was exported. Exports of butter increased from 10 000 tons in1926 to 23 500 tons in 1938. In terms of the amount of exported butter, Latvia was fourth in Europe in 1938. Latvia's clean and unpolluted environment guaranteed healthy dairy products and still does so.

Agriculture

Approximately 15% of all the people who are employed in the Latvian economy work in agriculture. The largest proportion is crop-farming. Latvia produces enough milk to satisfy domestic demand for milk and dairy products. Latvia's climate is appropriate for cultivation of highly productive and economically effective meadows, pastureland and perennial pasture grasses, which makes it possible to develop livestock breeding, and especially dairy farming. Grain farming produces enough to satisfy local demand including a share of livestock, dairy and poultry feed.

An investment project is being developed towards constructing the largest liquor distillery in the Baltic at *Jaunciems*, which would handle all the grain remaining after domestic demand in the Baltic States. Large-scale farms produce a good grain crop with constant quality. Small farms lack the resources to bring the grain quality to the potential level of the particular variety of grain. Specialisation in varieties, modernisation of technology and increasing productivity is descriptive of sugar-beet production. There are two sugar factories in Latvia – in *Liepāja* and *Jelgava*.

Potatoes are grown mostly for local demand. They were first brought to Latvia during the reign of Duke Jacob of Kurzeme, and have become the *daily bread* for many today. Flax farming was developed in Latgale. A positive trend in Latvia's agriculture today is the rapid increase in specialised, non-traditional farms, which produce wild berries, mushrooms, different herbs, flowers and find good markets for their production.

Agriculture is one of the oldest forms of organised activity in Latvia. Land covered with forests were deforested and gave space to the cultivation of grain, vegetables and fruit. In the 18th century, the French ambassador to Stockholm wrote to his government: *The grain that is obtained in Vidzeme is better than grain from any other place… it can be stored for 8-10 years without fearing that it might become spoilt. No area in the world is more useful for storing up grain than Vidzeme.* France was also interested in the flaxseed that was grown in Latgale and the hemp grown in Kurzeme.

Flower Selection

There is a large garden in *Babīte* on the outskirts of Rīga, where visitors are bewildered by the diversity of smells in the spring. As one approaches the wave of pleasing smells, the diversity of rhododendron shapes and colours blinds the eyes. This is the home of professor Rihards Kondratovičs, a distinguished horticulturist and his son, associate professor Uldis Kondratovičs. They introduced rhododendrons to Latvia and created excellent varieties, including *Austra*, *Liesma* and *Polārzvaigzne*.

Latvians love flowers – the place of honour is always reserved for a flower porch in every homestead, Latvians bring flowers when visiting, they are popular decorations in the home and at work. During the period of the Soviet occupation, flowers were cultivated by both intellectuals and workers in Latvia. It was a source of extra income, a taste of market economy. The flowers and bulbs were usually sold by the growers themselves, but there were also dealers, who sold flowers and bulbs to Russia. The annual turnover was somewhere around 15 million pieces.

The boom in flowers promoted a growth in the cultivation of new varieties. Very soon, Latvians discovered that this was an area in which they could compete with the rest of the world. Today the work of Latvian horticulturists has set new standards for bulbous plants and other selected flowers throughout the world. Viktors Orehovs created Latvia's flower selection school and his lily varieties are still very popular. Pēteris Upītis, who is known as the father of flower selection in Latvia and his lilacs varieties *Zilaiskalns*, *Jaunkalsnavas nakts*, *Gaiziņkalns*, *Imants Ziedonis*, *Māte Ede Upīts*, and others. The name of Jānis Rukšāns is famous far beyond the frontiers of Latvia for his selected varieties of crocus, tulips, narcissus, and other flowers. Jānis Vasarietis is famous in West Europe for his day lilies. Tulips by V. Skuja and the 300 varieties of gladiola are grown around the globe.

The *Āraiši* windmill and miller's house, built in the 19th century and rebuilt in 1984. The windmill has a stationary base with revolving *top*. The wings of the windmill reach into the sky lofty and beautiful from *Dzirnavkalns* (Windmill hill) over the dreamy landscape with *Āraiši* village, Lake *Āraiši* and the ancient Latgallian lake castle from the 9th century down below

There are many mills preserved in Latvia. They are powered by wind and the power of water. There are different grades of milling. Some produce flour for simple, rough bread and livestock feed, while other grinds rye, wheat and corn into finer and cleaner flour without husks – flour that is used for white bread and other purposes. Milling may be accomplished with the help of both cylinder mills and millstone mills. Old Latvian mills may be seen not only in the Ethnographic Open-air Museum in Rīga, where they are collected from different parts of Latvia, but also in the Latvian countryside. There are still some hillocks with beautiful windmills standing and gently slicing the wind with their easy wings – a confirmation of the talents and skills of Latvian artisans.

However, today the large mills in Latvia handle purchasing, storing, processing, production of livestock feed, packaging and distribution. The stock company *Dobeles Dzirnavnieks* owns one of the largest mills in Latvia. The quality of SC *Dobeles Dzirnavnieks* products is guaranteed by the technical level of its equipment, the high quality of raw materials that are used and the supervision of the entire process with modern laboratory equipment. The annual turnover of the undertaking *Bauskas Klēts* is 1.15 million lats. The word *klēts* in its traditional sense is expanded when it comes to the operations of the undertaking. *Bauskas Klēts* not only processes and stores the grains, but also grinds it in its own mill and then with the flour that results produces bread and pastry products. The company produces 21 kinds of bread and more than 50 kinds of pastry products.

Baking Bread

The director of the company is master baker Normunds Skauģis, who produces the Latvian traditional rye bread known as *Lāču maize* ("Bear Bread"). It contains no yeast and no wheat flour, and is produced instead from roughly milled rye flour raised with natural leaveners in wooden troughs, shaped into loaves by hand and baked in wood-fire owns. The ancestors of Latvians always held bread in great reverence as they knew how much hard work was put into it before it came to the table. Bread is a gift from God and if one threw bread or even the crumbs on the ground, God would get angry and give no more. The widespread folk traditions were expressed as unwritten laws, which were obeyed without protest. Folk beliefs contain many instructions, as to what needs to be done so that the bread dough would rise well, because from well-risen dough, delicious bread would be baked. In order for the bread to rise well, it must be well kneaded. There is a folk belief that dough rises best if an angry and vicious person kneads it, therefore one must be angry while kneading the dough. A cross must be drawn on the first and the last loaves before putting them into an oven, so the bread is blessed and stays risen.

There is a wide selection of bread in Latvia. Every baker has his own professional secrets on how to produce best bread. The stock company *Hanzas Maiznīca* is the largest producer of bread in Latvia. Each day about 90 tons of bread is produced in their bakeries. The company employs 850 people. SC *Hanzas Maiznīca* produces more than 100 different breads and pastry products — rye bread, wheat bread, sour-sweet bread, cakes, pastries, and cookies, which are distributed to about 1500 stores.

Lakes

Latvia's lakes are beautiful, dotted with islands they rest in valleys below hills and forests, most are still clean, clear and unpolluted. Many species of freshwater fish live in the water, birds nest beside it and wild animals come to quench their thirst in it. Latvians have given beautiful names to the lakes – *Pulksteņu* ("Clock"), *Gulbju* ("Swan"), *Mežezers* ("Forest lake"), *Kausiņš* ("Little bowl"), etc. There is at least one, if not more legends or tales attached to every lake, mostly about how the lake came about and how it got its name. There are stories about sunken castles and many stories about flying lakes, which sometimes change their location. One tale tells that once upon the time, there were no lakes and God gave water to living creatures only through rain. He kept water in a large pearl, but once it was stolen by the devil. The devil did not have the key and could not open it. He became angry and threw the pearl against the ground. The pearl broke, and splashes of water gathered in valleys and holes and shone like little pearls.

There is a total of 2256 lakes in Latvia, which are larger than 1 hectare. They cover a total area of about 1000 square km or 1.5 % of the territory of Latvia. This does not include waterholes in swamps, ponds and small lakes. Latgale is richest in lakes – there are 273 lakes in *Krāslava* district, 194 lakes in *Daugavpils* district and 183 lakes in *Rēzekne* district. There are considerably fewer lakes in the Zemgale region – 8 in *Bauska* district and 9 in *Jelgava* district. There are local groups and systems of lakes. The largest Latvia's lakes are found in Latgale – Lake *Lubāna* (82 km2), Lake *Rāzna* (57.8 km2). The deepest lake, too, is found in Latgale – Lake *Drīdzis* (65.1 m). Lake *Drīdzis* is the deepest lake in the Baltic. The deepest part of the lake is found in the middle of the lake, although the average depth of the lake is only 12.8 m. Lake *Garais* is the second deepest lake in Latvia – 56 m with the average depth of 16.5 m. Lake *Ežezers* (also called *Ješa*, *Ješu* or *Ieša*) has the greatest number of islands and it, too, is in Latgale. There is no record of the exact number of islands. New islands appear as the water level drops and disappear as the level rises again. The greatest number of islands ever recorded is 100.

The Abava River Valley

The *Abava* River valley, created by the *Abava* River, is 1 – 2 km across and up to 30 m deep. It formed during the end of the last Ice Age as water from a melting glacier sought its way to the Baltic Sea. The part of the valley between *Kandava* and *Renda* is a nature reserve. The purpose for the reserve is to preserve rare and unique elements of the natural environment. Similar reserves protect the rocky part of Vidzeme seashore, the *Salaca* River valley, Lake *Drīdzis* and the surrounding landscape, the *Venta* River valley, Lake *Svente*, etc. The *Imula* and *Amula* rivers flow into the *Amata* River in the territory of the reserve. Layers of dolomite and sandstone from Devonian period are exposed in the two river valleys as well.

The many caves formed in the walls and slopes of the valleys are objects of interest. For example, *Māras kambari* ("Māra's chambers") – three narrow caves on the right side of the valley's slope 6 km upstream from Renda. There are reasons to believe it was an ancient sacred place. The *Laupītāju* ("Robbers") cave is located near *Māras kambari* on the right side of the river valley. It is 11.5 m long, 2.2 m high and 2.5 m wide. A stream flows out the cave. The name of the cave comes from tales about hidden treasure in the cave. The 6.7 m long and 1.6 m high *Velnala* ("Devil's Cave") is located 7 km downstream from *Kandava*.

The *Abava* River turns into rapids and a 35 m wide and 0.5 m high waterfall – *Abavas rumba* 4 km downstream from Sabile.

The landscape in the *Abava* River valley is very spectacular. The leaves of the trees in the valley tone especially beautiful after the first autumn frosts. Many streams and creeks flow through the *Abava* River valley. In 1991, a stone plaque called the symbol of Earthly balance, a plaque of prayer to Mother Earth with symbols for four human races was placed next to the highway to *Sabile*. Newly wed couples often stop here to receive blessing from Mother Earth.

Vīna ("Wine") Hill, mentioned as the northernmost vineyard in the Guinness Book of Records, is located near *Sabile* (first mentioned in historical documents in 1253). Name *Sabile* comes from an interpretation of the sound of a rolling church bell. Vineyards were here during the rule of the Livonian Order. Wine from Sabile was a popular export. Most vineyards were lost after World War II.

Amata – the affluent of the Gauja River in Cēsis district

Amata – the Rapid Trout River

The *Amata* River is one of the small Latvian rivers, described by Latvians with a saying: it runs tinklingly. The *Amata* River runs tinklingly with rapid, clear and clean water. It meanders in a deep, eroded bed with steep banks. It is 67 km long and it falls 193 m (2.84 m/km). The lower valley has steep sandstone and dolomite sides, up to 45 m in some places. It is one of the deepest and most unique river valleys in the territory of the *Gauja* National Park.

There are many large cliffs and rock along the sides of the river: *Zvārte*, *Vizuļi*, *Ķaubji*, *Dzilna*, *Incēnu Dambis*, *Migla* Rock, *Dolomīti*, *Ainava* Bluff, etc. *Ainava* Bluff with *Birzene* and *Ainava* rocks is located 200 m downstream from *Kārļa* Bridge and is one of the highest bluffs in Latvia with a great view over the *Amata* River valley. There are many rapids in the *Amata* River. A section of almost continuous waterfalls and rapids starts downstream from *Ieriķi - Gulbene* railway bridge. The largest rapids are those of *Lustūža*, *Smīde* and *Dolomīta*. The *Amata* River has many tributary rivers – the *Melnupe*, *Pieņupe*, *Vilkate*, *Raganiņa*, *Dadžupe*, *Pērļupe* and *Nediene* rivers. The *Nediene* River washed away the *Zēģeri* mill's dam several times and the local people experienced days of trouble as the name of the river indicates in Latvian.

Salmon and other fish that like clean and turbulent waters live in the *Amata* River. Traditional canoeing competitions take place in the *Amata* River every spring during the period of flooding. Many men and women come to test their enthusiasm and zest for life in the cold water (+4° to +8°C).

Fishing

The Kolka Lighthouse

Latvian fishermen hauling in a heavy catch

A lighthouse was built on an artificial island put on a sandbar 5 km from *Kolkasrags* (*Kolka* horn) in 1883 – 1884. The boulders for construction work were transported from *Bažu* swamp on sledges by the local farmers. The first steam whistle in Russia was installed in the lighthouse. The lighthouse functions automatically since 1985.

Kolka is a fishing village in the *Dungada* district. *Koklasrags* is the northernmost extension of land in Kurzeme. Place-names, which include – *rags*, may usually be associated with meanings such as "headland", "cape" or "sandbar". *Kolkasrags* is about 7 km long sandbar with dolomite core about 2 m from the surface. These are very dangerous waters to navigate in. Countless shipwrecks lay scattered around the sandbar, because 7 m high waves crash against one another here during storms.

There are legends, which tell that torches were lit during the storms in order to direct ships away from the sandbar. However, the same trick was sometimes used by pirates to direct the ships on to the sandbar. The ships were then plundered, and the sailors were killed. Therefore the Liv name *kuolka*, meaning *await death* or *die*, was given to the place. The sandbar, also been called *the nose of the evil giant Tom*, separates the Baltic Sea from the Gulf of Rīga, called the *Little Sea* by the Kurs. One may experience a peculiar feeling by stand in different seas with each foot. A mirage of *Roņu* Island is sometimes visible from *Kolkasrags*.

Bale-fire lifted on special plates guided ships until 1787. There were two small lighthouses, which are now nothing but ruins.

There are many lighthouses along the coastline of Latvia, guiding sailors and fishers. The northernmost lighthouse is in *Ainaži*, the southernmost one – the *Pape* lighthouse.

Latvia has about 500 km of shoreline. There are some 3200 lakes, many rivers and creeks. Fishing is one of the most developed food industry sectors in Latvia with ancient traditions. Early settlers in Latvia fished already 4000 years ago. Fishermen are mentioned in the Chronicles of *Indriķis*, fishermen are named in many Latvian folksongs. The first fisherman's association was founded in Riga in 1220. Only fresh fish was sold in markets in Riga until the 15th century, later – smoked and salted fish as well. The first canneries appeared in 1884.

Manufacturers in Riga presented a new product called *Šprotes eļļā* (Sprats in oil) in 1891. The product has kept its position on international markets right up to today. Three canneries exported their production to all of the world's continents in 1939. Latvians have always loved offshore fishing, which was the principal occupation of the people in the fishing villages. Open-sea fishing rapidly developed in the more open parts of the Baltic Sea. Holiday fishing and leisure fishing as tourist activities developed in some fishing villages. Standing traps for pilchard, creels, nets and towlines are the most frequently used fishing tools in the Baltic Sea, in coastal waters – mostly fishnets. The fishing stock is being restored in Latvia. More salmon and trout is being bred here than in any other country along the Baltic Sea. Latvia is one of the few European countries where salmon spawn in the wild, in rapid creeks in Vidzeme and Kurzeme. The popular delicacy crayfish live in Latvian lakes and rivers. Lamprey is found in the *Daugava* River and the *Gauja* River.

The Sea Coast of Kurzeme

The Sea Coast of Vidzeme

The second largest recreation area with sandy beaches and pine forests is located north-east of Rīga, between *Vecāķi* and *Saulkrasti*. The most spectacular part of Vidzeme sea coast starts from the Age River sea port. The shore is covered with a "pavement" of rocks and boulders. Rocks of varied size are also found in water, some resemble giants with seaweed beards. The protected boulder at Skulte appeared only in 1853. The most colourful and spectacular part is the sea coast around the *Vitrupe* River delta. The *Svētupe* ("Sacred") River reaches the sea between the *Vitrupe* and *Salaca* rivers. The caves along the *Svētupe* River were used for sacred sacrificial rituals by the ancient Livs, but the echo in the *Drūmās* ("Gloomy") Cliffs is comparable with that in *Skaņaiskalns* ("Clarion Hill") of the *Salaca* River. Right near the Estonian border can be found the *Salaca* River and the landscape of *Zilaiskalns* ("Blue Hills") and Lake *Burtnieki*. *Salacgrīva* was a major exporting port in the late-19th century, almost as significant as Rīga port. It is now a fishing port. *Ainaži* is notable for the first maritime college in Latvia, founded by one of the first well-educated Latvians, Krišjānis Valdemārs in 1864.

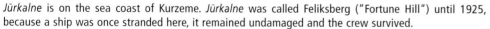

Jūrkalne is on the sea coast of Kurzeme. *Jūrkalne* was called Feliksberg ("Fortune Hill") until 1925, because a ship was once stranded here, it remained undamaged and the crew survived.
There are no mountains, high cliff walls, high waterfalls in Latvia; the landscape of our country is balanced and placid. But Latvia always has a changing, turbulent sea. The sea coast of Kurzeme is unique, just as the sea coast of Vidzeme is. A wavy dune rises to quite some distance from the sea near *Pape*, *Puze* and *Ugāle*. This was the sea coast, which once upon a time stood against the crashing waves. North of windy Liepāja, the Baltic Sea coast becomes steeper and sand cliffs appear. A most impressive sea coast starts from *Pāvilosta*. Here the sea demonstrates its awesome power by gnawing its way into the mainland and forming steep cliffs. The highest ones are at *Jūrkalne*.
There is an ancient site of shipwrecks in the sea near *Kolkasrags*. In 1883, a lighthouse was build here on an artificial island put on the further end of a sandbar. *Slītere* forest stretch along the coastline and pines cover the coastal dunes. The *Slītere* reserve is located in this area and nature is well preserved here. Further south of the *Engure* bird reserve, stretch the sandy plains and swamps of Rīga district, moorland, pine forests, and *Jūrmala* beach – the most popular recreation areas in Latvia.

Autumn Paints Latvia in Most Spectacular Shades

The Republic of Latvia is located in temperate climate zone on the coasts of the Baltic Sea and the Gulf of Rīga. The level terrain of the country presents no obstacles to the movement of weather fronts. West winds dominate. There is an average of 160 – 180 cloudy days per year in Latvia. The frost-free period of the year is shorter in the Vidzeme highlands. It also receives more precipitation than the plains.

September, October and November are the autumn months of the year. The transition from summer to autumn is slow and steady, which makes it less obvious. A winter crop is harvested in August, the spring crop – in September. Rye and wheat is sown at this time, too. No delay of harvesting is acceptable, because autumn is a rainy season in Latvia. First frosts come in September – first in north-eastern Latvia, then the central regions, and finally, in late September, the coastal areas are reached. Nature bursts into a bloom of colour. The Vidzeme

highlands, often called Vidzeme's Switzerland, provides especially beautiful views. However, the colourful beauty does not last long, because the dominating south-western winds bring long periods of rain, cloudy days, fog (especially in plains), and the average temperature in September is +10° to +13°C, in October – from +5° to 8°C. Storms are quite common. Potatoes and beets are gathered in autumn.

The temperature starts to drop. Water freezes over in November and the first snow starts to fall. The average temperature drops between +3° and -1°C and the first layer of snow builds up. Latvians forecast approaching frosts by observing the processes in nature, the behaviour of animals and birds. If migrating birds fly high and in a hurry, – frost is near. If a rooster stands on one leg, – it will be cold. If moles dig in late autumn, – winter will be cold and spring will come late. Latvian folk beliefs also say that, if autumn is nice, winter will be nice, too.

Angling

People in Latvia fish both for leisure and for sports, using the tools of an angler to catch fish. Latvian law specifies areas of dry land along shores of bodies of water where fishing is permitted. The zone is 4 m wide along privately owned waterways (and the law requires there to be a sign saying *Private* on the property), while in the case of other waterways the zone measures 10 to 20 m in width. Anglers require a license. The official period during spring when fishing is prohibited applies to trout, pike, perch, salmon, and other fish. There are limits to how many of fish species specimens are allowed to be caught by an angler within a 24-hour period. Today the oldest angling club is called *Salmo* and brings together anglers of salmon and trout. Fly anglers have their own club, and each October they organize an international fly-fishing competition on the *Gauja* River. The *Pacere* organization, which specializes in trout, is also active in working on programmes, which aim to protect fish population. During the spring, summer and autumn anglers use various kinds of fishing poles, and spinning gear, while during the winter ice fishing is popular. Closed private ponds and small lakes are becoming increasingly common in Latvia. These are known as *angler's paradise*, because anglers are allowed to pull out large carps or rainbow trout and keep them for a certain fee.

Executive Gunārs Ķirsons organizes a competition every year, The Large Fish of Latgale on Lake *Lubāns*. Anglers, by invitation, catch fish – usually large pike – mark them and release them back into the water. The most excellent angling trophies in Latvia are: pike – 19.56 kg, catfish – 56.2 kg, stream trout – 3.05 kg, rainbow trout – 6.66 kg, carp – 19.7 kg. Latvian angler stories are very much like those of any other country.

Hunting

There are some 34 000 registered hunters in Latvia, united in 974 clubs and organisations. The Hunting Law determines the basic principles of hunting game. Issues concerning how hunts are to be held and what kinds of animals can be hunted are determined by Cabinet regulations. Animals that can be hunted in Latvia are moose, stages, deer, wild pigs, wolves, foxes, lynxes, badgers, racoons, forest martens, American mink, beavers, rabbits, white-fronted geese, ducks, coots, wood-cocks, common snipes, wood pigeons, hazel grouses, capercaillye and black grouse cockerels, ravens, crows and magpies.

The animals common in Latvia provide high quality trophies, and trophy contests are often held. Hunters take special interest in acquiring information about animal population sizes and conditions in hunting areas. Animals are fed, their habitats are improved, and measures are taken to avoid damage to agriculture and forestry. Together with the State Forestry Service, hunters count animal populations. Regulations in Latvia permit several kinds of hunting, including work with dogs, use of hunting devices (traps), from boats and with beaters. The latter kind of hunting is most popular in Latvia, because it allows many hunters to come together, spend a nice day out hunting, and then gather around supper table to tell hunter's stories. Latvian hunters wish each other: *No down, no feather!*

Cliffs and Rocks in Latvia

Zvārte Rock, located on the left bank of the *Amata* River is the most spectacular sandstone rock in Latvia. It is bent in a semi-circle and consists of two parts: a vertical cliff nose (height - 20 m) and a semi-circular slope. The combined height of the cliff is 150 m.

The *Amata* River valley upstream from the bridge over the river on Rīga - Pskow highway forms steep slopes. Downstream from *Kārļi*, the *Amata* River has eroded its way into layers of sandstone. The river valley is more than one km wide and more than 50 m deep. The sides of the river valley are closed in by several tens of meters of sandstone walls, one of which is called *Zvārtes* Rock. The depth of the valley reduces to 20 m and the cliffs are lower downstream. The landscape is very beautiful; the valley is covered with forests and gorgeous meadows in clearings.

There are many cliffs and rocks on the banks of *Amata* River – the *Iļāku, Kaubju, Dambja, Stūķu, Vanagu* rocks, the spectacular *Ainavu* cliff with a wide view over the *Amata* River valley. There are open sandstone rocks in the valleys of the *Rauna* and *Brasla* rivers, but there are no dolomite rocks. The *Gauja* River valley is richest in open rocks, most of which are steep – the *Miglu, Liepu, Kazu, Cīrulišu, Launaga* and other rocks, which have eloquent names in spoken Latvian. Many tales and legends are attached to the caves along the *Gauja* River – the *Ērgļu, Līņu, Kūķu, Velna* caves. A beautiful landscape opens up around *Skaņais* Hill and in combination with ones voice, an impressive echo is created.

The "crying" travertine rocks in *Cēsu* district along the right bank of the *Rauna* River – *Rauna Staburags*

Raudošās ("crying") Rocks

The travertine rock at the *Rauna* River, called the *Little Staburags* by the local people, started to form some 8000 years ago. The process continues as the limestone sediments carried by small streams are deposited over the rock. The rock is 17 m long and 2 – 3.5 m high. There is a 1.3-m long bowl 1.1-m above the ground, where water carried by streams gathers. The combined height of the rocks is 35 m. *Rauna Staburags* is the only known place in Latvia, where Alpine butterwort grows – an endangered plant in Latvia. The landscape is very beautiful here. The *Rauna* River is one of the small and rapid rivers in Latvia. In some places, it descends at 9 m per km. The banks of the *Rauna* River are 3 – 10 m high, rocky or slowly descending. The river meanders through forested areas and ravines, trout and salmon are found here.

Unfortunately, the largest and most beautiful of the "crying" rocks – the Great *Staburags* or the *Daugava Staburadze* was flooded by *Pļaviņu* Hydroelectric station (HES). The rock was located on the *Daugava* River 1 km downstream from *Vīgante* and 9 km upstream from *Koknese*. The site of *Staburags* may only be recognised by the stairs leading to the waterfront of the dam of *Pļaviņu* HES. The 18.5-m high freshwater limestone *Staburags* rock is found deep below the surface. *Staburadze* is the symbol of "crying" rocks in Latvian poetry and mythology. Many Latvian writers describe it in their works. The legend about the *Daugava* River says: Once a young man went fishing in the *Daugava* River. His bride stayed on the bank. Suddenly, massive waves appeared out of nowhere and sank the boat along with the young man. The poor bride stayed on the bank for days and nights, crying and asking the *Daugava* River to have mercy and release her beloved one. She never stopped crying and turned into a rock – *Staburadze* rock.

Winter in Latvia lasts three to five months on average – from the middle of November to the beginning of March. Frost becomes permanent in the beginning of December in eastern parts of the country, and in the middle of the month in the western parts. The land freezes and snow starts to fall in November, followed by thaws, when temperature is about 0°C. Temperature usually changes rather often in December, too. Periods of frost are followed by thaws, snow, – by rain. Fog, rime and drizzle are common at this time of year. Winter comes slow in Latvia. The average temperature in coastal areas is –2° to –3°C, while –7°C in the eastern districts. The lowest temperatures may be observed in January and February, when the eastern winds bring cold, continental air from Eastern Europe. Sometimes the temperature drops as low as

–30°, –40°C. February is called the *putenis* (snowstorm) month in Latvia. There is an average of seven days of snowstorms every winter. The weather is mildly cold, often cloudy. The snow cover is about 20-30 cm thick in western districts and 30-50 cm in eastern parts. One may ski and skate all winter long, especially on *Gaiziņš* Hill and the surrounding areas. The snow cover starts to melt in late March, while the beginning of the month is still mildly cold with temperatures often below 0°C. Latvians forecast weather of the following seasons in winter, too, from observing natural processes: *If February is often foggy, – the rest of the year will be rainy. If cows moult early, – spring will come early.*

Railway bridge – the bridge across the *Daugava* River was inaugurated in 1914. It was built on 10 supports. The busbar near the right side of the river served as a drawbridge to let ships through. The bridge was demolished during World War I, and it collapsed into the river. The bridge was restored after the war. The new bridge served until World War II, when both the bridge and its supports were destroyed. Work on the new bridge was started already at the end of 1944. A provisional wooden bridge was built first. The iron bridge was completed in 1951.

Construction of narrow gauge railways was started some hundred years ago during the rule of the Tsars. The distance between the rails is 650 and 750 mm. Latvians used to joke that the different standards is a security measure against enemy intervention in case a war broke out between the neighbouring parishes. During the period up to World War II, narrow gauge railways, nicknamed *mazbānītis*, connected almost all of the largest cities in Latvia. It was also an important means of transportation for passengers and cargo during the post-war period.

Now only one little locomotive hauls carriages along the last remaining narrow gauge railway, which connects *Alūksne* and *Gulbene*. Once it was a common sight in every district just like the water towers, which supplied water to the steam engines. The advantages of *mazbānītis* over other means of transportation were always appreciated by the people in rural areas. It was a convenient way to go to the nearest city, the neighbouring parish to pick wild berries and mushrooms or to pay a visit to departed relatives at a cemetery.

Everybody feels at home here, because most passengers know each other and even the conductors and drivers are local people, who usually stay on the job for many years and learn all their passengers and their habits. The driver would never slam the door in front of a late mushroom or wild berry picker. The passengers, in their turn, would always assist the driver in case a fallen tree blocked the tracks. *Mazbānītis* is more than just means of transportation, it is a lifestyle, some what like a religion. If the funding is cut for the servicing of the old engines, carriages, and tracks, a bright and colourful page in the history of Latvia will be lost along with the narrow gauge railway.

The bridge across the *Rauna* River – the highest railroad bridge in Latvia. It is 24 m above the river

Valmiera

Saint Simon Church

The city – the heart of Vidzeme, the industrial, economic, educational and cultural centre of Vidzeme. A city which already in 1323 had gained the rights of a city. In truth, in the territory of *Valmiera* since the 10th century there had existed the *Autīne* lettgalian hill-castle, which is mentioned in the Chronicle of Indriķis. In the 13th century, a brick and stone castle was erected here by the Order of the Sword, surrounding which a settlement of craftsmen and traders was established. In different centuries the name of the city was written differently: *Wolmaria*, *Wolmahr*, *Wolmar*, *Waldemer*. From the 14th to 16th centuries, *Valmiera* was a Hansa city. After the 1793 administrative reforms *Valmiera* became a county centre. Through *Valmiera* passed the postal route established during the Swedish rule that joined St. Petersburg with Rīga and Western Europe.

In 1741, the first Vidzeme teacher's seminar was established in *Valmiera*. In 1802, an anti-feudal peasant's movement arose from the *Valmiera* congregation that is now known as the *Kaugaru* rebellion. The name of *Valmiera* is also associated with the Herrnhuter movement, when in the congregations of the Brethren the aspirations of Latvians for education were strengthened, books were written and re-written, and Latvians learnt to be industrious, wise and educated. In the 19th century *Valmiera* was the only city in Latvia where all the city councillors were Latvian. The chief doctor of Valmiera, Georgs Apinis was for many years the mayor of the city, as well as an entrepreneur who built the city hospital. The 18th and 19th century buildings of the city centre were destroyed in the Second World War.

In 1963, a fibre-glass factory was built in *Valmiera*, which now is a public stock company. Its products are an important part of Latvia's exports. The Latvian-Australian joint venture a/s *Valpro Korp*, which produces petrol cans and heating boilers also exports a large amount of its production. The main food processors are a/s *Vidzemes piens* and *Sviesta siera eksports*, and the Latvian-German joint venture SIA *Valmieras maiznieks*. The interests of entrepreneurs are represented by one of Latvia's most influential entrepreneur associations, *Ozols*. *Valmiera* has the largest hospital in Vidzeme. The Vidzeme University was established in 1996. *Valmiera* is one of the most looked after cities in Latvia with clean parks and gardens and mowed lawns. The *Valmiera* theatre ensemble travels all over Latvia with its always excellent productions and has become one of Latvia's most popular theatre troupes.

Monument to the boys of *Valmiera*, heroes of the books by Pāvils Rozītis

The Inčukalns Underground Gas Storage Facility - a Unique Geological Formation, which Allows Storing Natural Gas During Summer and Supplies Consumers in Latvia, Lithuania, Estonia and Western Russia During Winter

There are very few underground gas storage facilities in the world the like of that at *Inčukalns*. Most of the natural gas pumped to Latvia from Russia during months of summer and early autumn is stored in the *Inčukalns* underground gas storage facility. It has been in operation since 1968. The facility can store up to 4 billion cubic meters of gas, including 2.15 billion cubic meters of buffer gas. Enormous compressors are used to pump the gas into porous sandstone rock that is 700 meters under the ground and is surrounded on all sides by clay and dolomite through which the gas cannot pass. During the winter, the storage facility provides gas to consumers in Latvia, Estonia, Lithuania and Western Russia. The facility is completely safe and ecological research has shown that it has no deleterious effect on the surrounding environment, air and groundwater. The gas supply system has developed from a simple pipeline network into

a computerised system monitored and operated by software programmes. The control centre of the *Inčukalns* underground gas storage facility provides uninterrupted and precise gas supply to the Baltic States and Western Russia. The Rīga liquid gas export facility has port facilities, which allow SC *Latvijas Gāze* to provide stevedore services as well.

The *Snēpele* underground gas storage facility (capacity – 17.5 million cubic meters) is another gas storage facility, which is similar to the one in *Inčukalns*. There are also similar facilities at *Aizpute* (16 million cubic meters), *Dobele* (10 million cubic meters), *Ziemeļblīdene* (9 million cubic meters), and elsewhere. Latvia's underground gas storage facilities could theoretically provide gas to most of the continent of Europe for an entire winter, thus overcoming the gasification problem in Europe.

Energy. VAS Latvenergo

Plavinas HES is the largest hydroelectric station in the Baltic States with a total output of 870 megawatts. Construction was begun in 1961 and it was an important project in very difficult geological circumstances – on moraine sandstone, with which the ancient bed of the *Daugava* is filled. The Plaviņas HES includes a water overflow and the whole hydro-works complex is compact

In the 1960s on the *Daugava* the *Plaviņas* HES was built and nearby the new city of *Aizkraukle* was established. The newest of the large *Daugava* hydroelectric stations is located nearly on the boundaries of the City of Rīga. The lower reaches of the *Daugava* does not have steep banks, therefore the reservoirs formed by the HES covers a wide territory and are often called the *Rīga* HES sea.

At this time the construction of various types of small and medium-sized energy sources has become topical. Small hydroelectric stations and combined heat and power stations are being built, as well as wind rotors are being erected. Small and medium energy efficient projects in Latvia are realised by the Energy Efficiency Fund, which supports them with low-interest credits. The Fund resources are formed from European Union Phare programme funding with a total of 3.6 million Euro, funds from the *Latvijas Hipotēku un Zemes Banka*

[Latvian Mortgage and Land Bank] and funds from the Latvian State budget which are allocated for this purpose.

Latvia is not rich in energy resources, its richness lies in the forests, peat, the force water and wind. Domestic resources cover 20%-40% of the State energy consumption, the rest is imported fossil fuels. The consumption of gas and wood grows each year, but the use of environmentally unfriendly black oil is reduced. The climate and the quality of construction determine the usage of energy resources in the Latvian economic structure. Heating uses 40%, industry about 20%, transport about 20% and electricity generation about 11% of energy resources. A/s *Latvijas Gāze* ensures the supply of natural gas and compressed gas to the inhabitants and undertakings of Latvia, but 98% of the amount of electricity needed for the Latvian economy is supplied by VAS *Latvenergo*.

The Progress of the Latvian National Armed Forces towards NATO

In constant readiness to defend the Latvian State – army, navy and air forces

The task of the National Armed Forces (NAF) is to ensure the security of the Latvian State and its inhabitants, the territorial integrity of the State, to prevent and eliminate external and internal threats to the State and to take part in peacekeeping operations in other states. The rebirth of the Latvian Armed Forces can be taken to be the barricade days of 1991, when people from all over Latvia came to defend Parliament and the Government. On 21 August 1991, Latvia regained its independence and the men of Latvia did not delay in organising the National Guard (*Zemessardze*) and the Border Guard. The National Guard is the largest structure in the National Armed Forces and was established on 23 August 1991.

The foundation of the defence of the territory of Latvia are the land forces which also includes the National Guard. The main tasks of the land forces is to secure the defence of the land territory of Latvia, to prepare combat-ready army units, to take part in international peacekeeping operations, as well as emergency and rescue work, and the elimination of the consequences of extraordinary situations. In order to successfully take part in international peacekeeping missions, LATBAT – the Latvian battalion was formed in 1999.

The Latvian Navy secures the territorial integrity of Latvia's sea-borders, find and eliminates dangerous explosive objects in the sea, as well as takes part in ecological supervision and search and rescue operations at sea.

The tasks of the Latvian Air Force is the observation, control and defence of Latvian air space, to provide assistance in the elimination of the consequences of natural disasters and others. The development of the NAF is concentrated in two directions – increasing the self-defence potential and capability of the State, as well as ensuring the compatibility of the NAF with the armed forces of NATO states.

Immediately after the regaining of independence, Latvia expressed its desire to join the North Atlantic Treaty Organisation – NATO. Since the end of the Cold War NATO has established several programmes in which states that are not members of NATO also take part. One of the largest is the Partnership for Peace (PfP) programme with which Latvia has been involved since 1994. Since 1996, Latvia also participates in NATO led peacekeeping operations. The professionalism of our soldiers has highly rated on many occasions.

Yachts

Latvians have long been known as skilful navigators, therefore sailing has long traditions in Latvia. The first yacht club in Rīga was founded in 1878 and was located in *Balasta dambis* 1. The first yacht competition took place in the same year on the *Daugava* River. Seven yachts took part. The Lake *Ķīšezers* yacht club was founded in 1913 in Rīga with 331 members, 68 yachts and 6 iceboats. In 1933, there were already 9 associations with a total of 317 yachts. Latvian contestants actively took part in international regattas. One of the most distinguished Latvian sports sailors, Jevgenijs Kanskis, was a prizewinner in both sailing on ice and in different categories of regular sailing. The Central yacht club was founded at the Lake *Ķīšezers* yacht station in 1946. It was relocated to *Bolderāja* in 1970. There were 152 yachts, windsurfing boards and other floating devices, 260 sailors, trained by 4 instructors. Sailors participated in different international competitions on regular basis. The sailor Aleksandrs Muzičenko won Olympic gold in the *Star* class.

Sailing has rapidly developed in Latvia during the last few years, mainly thanks to suitable conditions. Many yachts from other countries visit Latvia; international contacts are established and developed. There are 8 small ports of local significance – *Mērsrags*, *Pāvilosta*, *Salacgrīva*, *Skulte*, *Kolka*, *Engure*, *Kaiviži* and *Roja*. They handle about 1.5 % of the total cargo turnover in Latvia. They specialise in timber exports, handling of fish products, but they also have good prospects for developing into yacht tourism ports.

Airport Riga

Recently airport *Riga* has turned into one of the most advanced air traffic management centres in the world. The system of manoeuvring routes and runways has been restored.

The new airport building was constructed in 1999. Being modern and functional, it offers maximum comfort to the passengers and airport staff. Airlines connect Riga with almost all European countries. *British Airlines*, *Lufthansa*, *SAS*, *LOT* and other big international companies make flights to Riga.

In the beginning of 2001 fourteen Latvian air carriers offered their services in Latvia. Two of them made regular flights, but twelve – irregular. Mostly they deal with passenger transport. For the present there is no demand for inland flights, therefore all flights are international. 89% of all passengers travel by regular flights. The irregular airlines are characterised by longer average flight distances per one passenger. The number of passengers increases steadily year by year. More and more people use Latvian airlines (48%). *Air Baltic* takes the leading position among Latvian companies regarding the number of passengers. Through constant development *Air Baltic* has become a highly professional company.

In 1992 Latvia ratified the International Convention of Civil Aviation and became a full – fledged member of the International Organisation of Civil Aviation. Latvia has taken a leading place in the European region of Civil Aviation. At present Latvia is planning to join the Organisation of Safety of European Air Navigation and is already taking part in some of its programmes.

British Airways – the smoothest connection between Riga and London in 21st century

Europe's largest airline offers five flights a week between London and Riga. It is the fastest and smoothest way from the Latvian capital to London and further on to more than two hundred *British Airways* destinations world-wide.

British Airways is the biggest carrier between Riga and North America. Over the years, it has sustained its leadership in this market segment with average of 25 % of passengers flying via London on its routes to the USA and Canada. Recently this position has been strengthened by introducing the first ever seats that can be easily converted into completely flat beds on long-haul flights in the airline business class Club World.

The seats are designed in forward and rearward facing pairs and configured to create a lounge style environment with 20 in the upper deck of a B747 and up to 50 in the main deck of B747s and B777s. Each armchair-like seat, complete with footstool, converts to a six-foot fully flat bed at the touch of a button. The unique lounge style layout is designed to maximise personal space and privacy, with each seat also featuring individual privacy screens which can be opened or closed dependent on whether customers are travelling alone. Traditional side-by-side seating is also available if customers prefer. *Lounge in sky* allows business passengers to sleep, work or relax at 35,000 ft.

The new product is part of the airline's biggest ever programme of product improvements and first of the kind in the industry's history.

Another innovation of the program is the introduction of a new class of travel for long-haul economy passengers called World Traveller Plus.

The unique new service is aimed at the cost conscious business traveller and discerning leisure passenger who want more space and privacy than in the World Traveller. It features a dedicated cabin, wider seats built by German-based racing car seat designer Recaro, the technology to work or relax.

In introducing the new service class *British Airways* has become the first major airline to offer four cabins for travel on a world-wide network.

These innovations along with improvements in all *British Airways* service classes will redefine business travel for the 21st century and set new industry benchmarks for comfort and innovation.

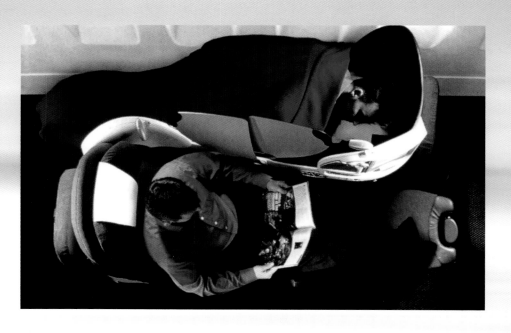

Laima

The first large industrial sweets undertakings in Latvia were established in the middle of the 19th century. In 1870, Teodors Rīgerts began the manufacture of chocolates in Rīga. His traditions were taken over in 1924 by the stock company a/s *Laima*, which increased production and sold its products not only in Latvia, but also in France, Britain, Scandinavia, USA and elsewhere. In 1881 the preserving and sweets factory L. W. Goegginger. The undertaking manufactured sweets, chocolates and biscuits, as well as various types of preserves. In 1940, both undertakings were nationalised and changed into confectionery factories. *Laima* retained its previous name, but the L. W. Goegginger factory was renamed *Uzvara* [Victory]. *Laima* specialised in chocolates, but *Uzvara* – in the manufacture of sugar confectionery.

In January 1998 a/s *Laima* merged with a/s *Uzvara*.

Laima offers its customers chocolates and ten varieties of chocolate sweets, and a wide range of various sugar confectioneries. A/s *Laima* products have received high praise in international exhibitions in Cologne, Moscow, St. Petersburg, Brno, Gdansk, Kiev, San Francisco, Alma-Ata, Vilnius, Tallinn and elsewhere. Today, *Laima's* products may be purchased not only in Latvia, but also in Lithuania, Estonia, Germany, the Czech Republic, Sweden, Canada, Israel, the USA and elsewhere.

On 24 November 2000, the a/s *Laima* stock control packet was purchased by a/s *Staburadze* – the second largest manufacturer of sweets in Latvia.

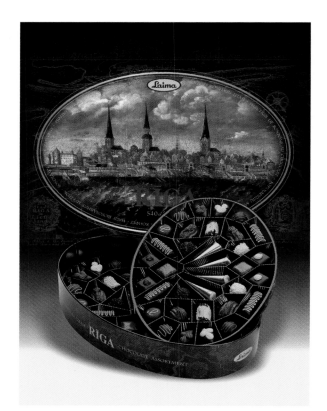

Staburadze

Staburadze is an undertaking with a long history and rich traditions. Its first name and history is closely associated with the Latvian entrepreneur Vilhelms Ķuze (1875-1941), who began to manufacture sweets already in 1910. During the First World War the firm was relocated to Russia and the manufacturing equipment was sold to the *Centrosojuz* company.

When Ķuze returned to Latvia in 1920, he renewed the undertaking. The products produced were sold in Latvia, as well as being exported to Europe, Sweden, North America, Australia and Asia. As recognition of the high quality and renown of its products the firm has receive the Grand Prix and other awards at international exhibitions and trade fairs in Antwerp, Paris and Brussels.

In 1940 the factory was nationalised and renamed 17 June in honour of the Russian Army which entered Rīga on 17 June 1940. During the Soviet period, the factory became popular throughout the Soviet Union.

After the restoration of Latvian independence in 1991, the undertaking was renamed *Staburadze*. Today the Staburadze control packet belongs to SIA *Nordic Food*. *Nordic Food* is a food company whose basis of success is the owner's extensive experience in the field of food manufacture and sales.

Staburadze is one of the leading confectionery manufacturers in Latvia, and offers wafer cakes, jelly sweets, wafers, biscuits, Swiss rolls and cakes.

Laima's Clock

Today's very popular clock on the corner of *Aspazijas* and *Brīvības bulvāris*, was erected in 1924 by the Social Democrat Mayor Vecvagars so that people would not be late for work. Initially the clock was located on a pole at the tram stop. Later it carried the name of the pioneer of chocolate-making in Latvia, Rīgerts, but in 1936 it became Laima's clock.

During the Soviet time, in the 1960s, it carried the slogans of *Miers, Peace, Frieden*.

However, now the name *Laima* is again in its old place and after its 1999 reconstruction, the clock both shows the correct time and reminds everyone of Latvia's largest manufacturer of chocolates, and, as before, serves as a popular place for rendezvous.

Banking and Financial System of Latvia

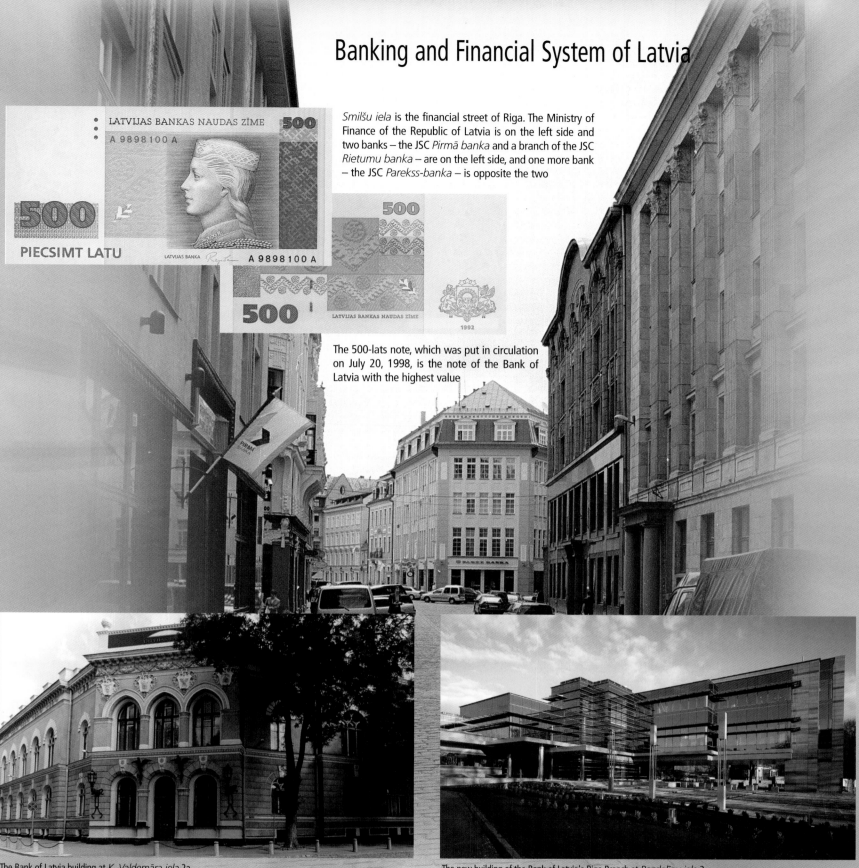

Smilšu iela is the financial street of Riga. The Ministry of Finance of the Republic of Latvia is on the left side and two banks – the JSC *Pirmā banka* and a branch of the JSC *Rietumu banka* – are on the left side, and one more bank – the JSC *Parekss-banka* – is opposite the two

The 500-lats note, which was put in circulation on July 20, 1998, is the note of the Bank of Latvia with the highest value

The Bank of Latvia building at *K. Valdemāra iela* 2a

The new building of the Bank of Latvia's Riga Branch at *Bezdelīgu iela* 3

The central bank is one of the symbols of a country. The Bank of Latvia was established in 1922 as an independent public institution with the right to issue the national currency. Ringolds Kalnings, who was Minister of Finance, was appointed Chairman of the Bank's Board of Governors. His successors to the post were Jūlijs Celms (appointed in 1926) and Ādolfs Klīve (appointed in 1931). The latter chaired the Board of Governors until the occupation of 1940. The Bank of Latvia was restored in 1990, and became a full-fledged central bank in 1991. Its status was reinforced by the Law *On the Bank of Latvia* of 1992. The Board of Governors, which is chaired by the Governor appointed by the Saeima of the Republic of Latvia, determines the Bank's monetary policy, takes interest rates decisions for Bank of Latvia asset and liability operations, and reviews and approves the annual budget of the Bank. Mr. Einars Repše, who was a member of the Monetary Reform Committee, has been the Bank's Governor since 1991. The Executive Board, whose members are chosen by the Board of Governors, manages the Bank's day-to-day activities. Mr. Ilmārs Rimšēvičs has been Chairman of the Executive Board since 1992; moreover, the Saeima has appointed him Vice-Governor of the Bank of Latvia. The Bank of Latvia is committed to promoting and maintaining a stable and efficient monetary and financial framework in the country. The Bank, together with advisors from Latvia and other countries, reintroduced the national currency. The first stage was the introduction of the Latvian ruble as a temporary currency, which served well in creating a stable financial environment and overcoming inflation, which accompanied economic reforms. The monetary reform ended with the reintroduction of the lats. The lats has proved to be a stable and trusted currency, contributing to the steady progress of the Latvian economy.

The building that houses the Bank of Latvia was designed by the Latvian architect Augusts Reinbergs (1860–1908). The building was put into operation in January 1905. It is one of the last eclectic buildings in Riga and is listed as a monument of national significance. Over time, the building has housed banks but the main bulding nowadays does not fully meet contemporary requirements for technical facilities and security of information and money resources, and its capacity is not adequate for the Bank's needs. In view of this, the Bank undertook the construction of a new building for its Riga Branch. To develop security standards and the design of the new building, the Bank sought the advice of experts from Germany. The foundation stone was laid on July 23, 1999, and the Bank of Latvia's new Riga branch work begun in the November of 2001.

British Chamber of Commerce in Latvia

Following on from informal business meetings in Latvia, a small group representing British companies and inward investors into Latvia agreed that the time was right to form a specific group to represent their interests. In March 1996 the British Chamber of Commerce in Latvia was officially established, offering a full range of services to members and other companies in Latvia and UK.

Members include leading names in British industry who have established offices or invested in Latvia, including British Airways, DHL, GlaxoWellcome, Shell, Unilever, BP, RMC Group, British Aerospace, UPS, PricewaterhouseCoopers, BSW Timber and ED&F Man.

Smaller companies, individual entrepreneurs and Latvian companies doing business with Britain are also represented.

Membership covers a wide range of sectors including Timber, Insurance, Transportation, Food, Construction and Property Development, Law and Accountancy.

From the experiences and knowledge of these members we are able to provide information and advice on doing business in and with Latvia.

The British Chamber of Commerce aim is to promote and encourage bilateral trade between Britain and Latvia and support the development of good business practice in Latvia. To further the development of trade and commerce between Britain and Latvia by promoting business transactions, offering advice and providing essential services. To advocate at all levels support for the continued development of principles of fair business practice and make representations on behalf of members.

The Chamber participates in lobbying on behalf of members on issues detrimental to investment in Latvia through the work with the Foreign Investors Council in Latvia. As well as the Joint Customs Business Board and the FIAS group proposing changes in legislation to ease administrative barriers to trade.

From the left: Vaira Vike-Freiberga, Edwards Bowen, Juris Benkis, Irish Ambassador, Douglas Balchin, Egons Pikelis, Imants Freibergs

The Chamber maintains a close working relationship with the British Embassy and other Chambers of Commerce in Riga, the Department of Trade and Industry and Trade Partners UK in the UK and the Latvian Development Agency. As a member of the Council of British Chambers in Continental Europe we gain access to some 8000 companies across the whole of Europe and the benefit of a wide range of information sources.

Shell History in the Baltic States

During the pre-war period, there were four *Shell Group* companies in the Baltic States: The *Shell Company of Estonia* Ltd. (established 9 July 1927); The *Shell Company of Lithuania* Ltd. (established 27 July 1927); *The Shell Company of Memel* Ltd. (established 1925), which became The *Shell Company of Klaipeda (Memel)* Ltd. on 27 July 1936; and the *Asiatic Petroleum Company (Baltic States)* Ltd. (established 23 August 1921), which became The *Shell Company of Latvia* Ltd. in July, 1927.

During this period, the *Shell* companies secured a strong position in the Baltic States, with a nearly fifty per cent share of the market. A network of more than 50 *Shell* service stations was established across the three countries.

During the pre-war period, petrol, kerosene, aviation fuel and some basic chemicals, such as white spirit dominated sales.

The Soviet Union expropriated the property of these companies in 1940, upon the annexation of the Baltic States. With the German advance into Russia, this property changed hands again, but control returned to the Soviet Union after the war. The companies in Lithuania and Latvia were thereafter dissolved, and *Shell Estonia* became *Shell East Europe Services Company* Ltd.

After 50 years of forced absence, *Shell* has returned to the Baltics. This return was preceded by a through investigation of business prospects and overall development in the Baltic States, and was manifested in 1993 with the establishment of three *Shell* companies: *Shell Eesti* AS, *Shell Latvia* SIA, and *Shell Lietuva* UAB.

When *Shell* establishes a company in any country, it is a sign of confidence that a sound business environment is evolving there.

Now there are 19 *Shell* service stations in Latvia: in the Riga, *Ventspils*, *Daugavpils* and *Bauska* regions.

Shell service stations in the Baltic States meet all of the technical, safety and environmental standards that are currently required in Western Europe. These stations are a modern, safe and convenient place for customers to buy fuel, lubricants, chemicals, car accessories and a range of other shop articles. *Shell* service stations offer a broad scope of technologically advanced equipment to make every visit as quick and pleasant as possible.

Shell service stations are environmentally sound. Some of the features which help to minimise damage to the environment include double-skinned tanks with electronically controlled gauges, equipment which eliminates vapours, plastic underground pipes which are resistant to corrosion, impermeable forecourts, leakage and evaporation detectors, effluent facilities and oil separators. *Shell* branded trucks, which have been constructed to meet Western safety and environmental standards, and which specially trained professional drivers drive deliver shell fuels.

Shell petrol stations strive to offer a wide variety of services in an attractive, safe and clean environment with friendly staff members to assist motorists in making the choice that is right for them.

The Embassy of the United States

The United States, which never recognized the forcible incorporation of Latvia into the Soviet Union, has maintained diplomatic relations with Latvia continuously since July 28, 1922. Following the renewal of Latvian independence, the United States opened its Embassy in September, 1991.

Under the direction of Ambassador Brian E. Carlson, who conducts diplomatic relations with the Republic of Latvia and coordinates the activities of the United States Government in Latvia.

During the summer of 1994, the President of the United States of America, Bill Clinton visited Latvia. During his stay the US President also visited the Latvian Stock Exchange

British Embassy

The Embassy, led by the Ambassador, Mr Stephen Nash, successfuly works with the Latvian authorities to fulfill bilateral political and economic relations with Latvia. It is implemented with help of regular meetings with members of the Latvian government, state officials, politicians and NGOS etc. Currently the main themes are UK-Latvia relations, Latvia's applications to join the EU and NATO, and Latvia's relations with Russia and Baltic co-operation.

Since Latvia regained its independence, Prince Charles has visited it twice. Photo: His Eminence during his second visit in November, 2001

The Canadian Embassy

The Canadian Embassy's main goal is assistance in communications and co-operation between Canada and the three Baltic States – Estonia, Lithuania, and Latvia. The three Embassy sections provide information about political and economic processes, support commercial links, as well as their establishment, and provide technical co-operation with Canada. The Embassy also gives support to Canadians who live in Estonia, Latvia, and Lithuania, or are planning to travel here, and assists people in the Baltic States who wish to visit Canada for tourist, business, educational, or immigration purposes.

In the lower floors of the building can be found the only commercial bank belonging to the Government of the Republic of Latvia – the *Hipotēku banka* (Mortgage Bank). This Bank is the moral heir of two commercial banks belonging to the Latvian Government from 1918 to 1940, the main activities of which were to provide loans to small and middle business, and mortgage credit. The Bank was founded by the Government in 1993, and the bank's future development model is to transform it into a classic Development Bank – a world recognised and proven government financial instrument, which is utilised to strengthen the state economy and for further growth.

The National Theatre and the Rīga City Council

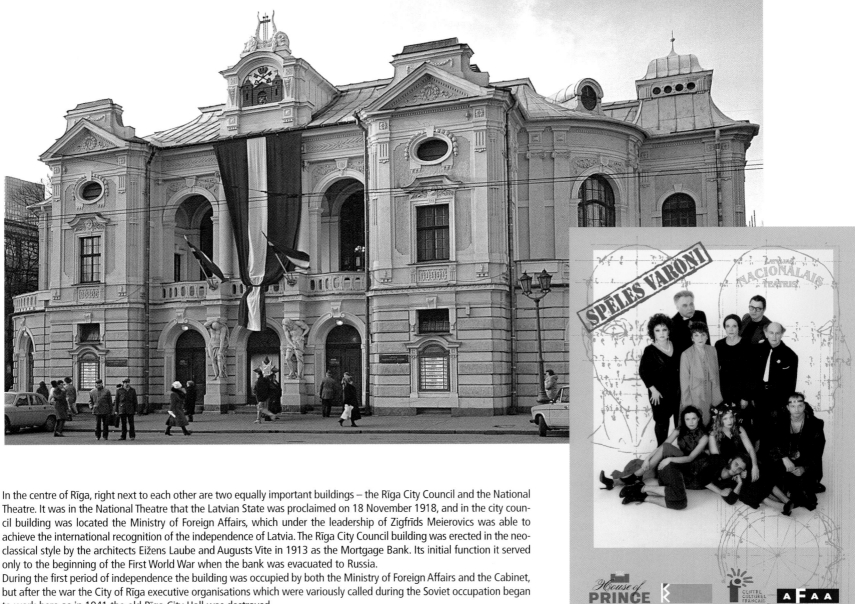

In the centre of Rīga, right next to each other are two equally important buildings – the Rīga City Council and the National Theatre. It was in the National Theatre that the Latvian State was proclaimed on 18 November 1918, and in the city council building was located the Ministry of Foreign Affairs, which under the leadership of Zigfrīds Meierovics was able to achieve the international recognition of the independence of Latvia. The Rīga City Council building was erected in the neoclassical style by the architects Eižens Laube and Augusts Vīte in 1913 as the Mortgage Bank. Its initial function it served only to the beginning of the First World War when the bank was evacuated to Russia.

During the first period of independence the building was occupied by both the Ministry of Foreign Affairs and the Cabinet, but after the war the City of Rīga executive organisations which were variously called during the Soviet occupation began to work here as in 1941 the old Rīga City Hall was destroyed.

Now 60 councillors and some 300 civil servants work in the Rīga City Council. Within the budget of the Rīga City Council, education, social welfare, erection of new buildings and restoration of old ones, maintenance of streets, city public transport and many other needs of the residents of the City of Rīga are ensured.

The National Theatre is a characteristic example of the eclecticism style that was erected in 1899-1902 based upon a project by A. Reinberg. The sculptural decorations on the facade were made by the sculptor A. Folc. The theatre seats 1928 people. In the 1970s, based upon a project by O. Dombrovskis, a small theatre with 100 seats and a café was built in the basement, where during the summer months guests are welcomed and served by the actors themselves. Initially it was the Second Rīga City theatre or Russian theatre.

Most popular Latvian author productions are plays by Rainis, Aspāzija, Brigadere, Blaumanis. Especially popular and beloved by the people is Blaumanis' *Skroderdienas Silmačos* [Days of the Tailor at *Silmači*], which is an irreplaceable part of the theatre's repertoire. The most outstanding National theatre productions postwar are from the world's classics: Tennessee Williams' *A Streetcar Named Desire* (1969), and Ferenc Molnár's *Liliom* and I. Jamiac's *Mr Hamilcar* (1981).

Culture and art has needed in all periods of time support from business structures. At the moment, for example, the general sponsor of the National theatre for the last five years has been the Danish undertaking *The House of Prince Rīga*, which is one of Latvia's largest and most stable undertakings, and the only manufacturer of tobacco products in Latvia. The undertaking has contributed each year significant financial resources for the development of the theatre, and in this way has promoted the cultural development of Latvia. Thanks to the support of the tobacco manufacturer, the best productions of the National theatre were created.

The Cabinet

Latvia is an independent, democratic republic. State power belongs to the people, and this power is expressed either directly or through elected representatives. The *Satversme* [Constitution] provides for both possibilities, and there are two sources of legislation – the *Saeima* and the people. The authority that the *Satversme* provides for the *Saeima*, the Cabinet and the President shows that Latvia is parliamentary republic. The Cabinet remains in office as long as the *Saeima* maintains faith in it. The government is to a certain extent independent from the *Saeima* in its work, but if the balance of power in the *Saeima* changes, the same usually happens in the Cabinet as well.

The President of Latvia is elected by the *Saeima* by a majority of the members of the *Saeima*.

The presidency in Latvia is largely a representative office, but the President has the right to summon emergency sessions of the *Saeima*, to summon and chair emergency meetings of the Cabinet, and to proclaim war.

Latvia's Constitution, known as the *Satversme*, was adopted by the first elected legislative body in Latvia – the Constitutional Assembly, which was elected in April 1920. The *Satversme* was adopted on 15 February 1922, and it came into force on 7 November of the same year. The *Satversme* was reinstated in phases after Latvia restored its independence in 1991. The *Satversme* was reinstated in full when the first freely elected post-Soviet 5th *Saeima* took office, on 6 July 1993.

An extraordinary meeting of the Cabinet. From the left: the Minister for the Interior, Māris Gulbis; the Minister for Finance, Valdis Dombrovskis; the Minister for Agriculture, Mārtiņš Roze; the Minister for Justice, Aivars Aksenoks; the Minister for Education and Science, Kārlis Šadurskis; the Minister for Foreign Affairs, Sandra Kalniete; Minister for Transport, Roberts Zīle; the Deputy Prime Minister, Ainars Šlesers; the Prime Minister, Einars Repše; the President of Latvia, Vaira Vīķe-Freiberga; the Minister for Defence, Ģirts Valdis Kristovskis; the Minister for Culture, Inguna Rībena; the Minister for Special Assignments – Children and Family Matters, Ainārs Baštiks; the Minister for Regional Development and Local Government Matters, Ivars Gaters; the Minister for Special Assignments – Health Care Matters, Āris Auders; the Minister for Environmental Protection and Regional Development, Raimonds Vējonis; the Minister for Economics, Juris Lujāns.

Unilever history

Unilever was formed in 1930 through the merger of the operations of the Dutch margarine company *Margarine Unie* and the British soap maker *Lever Brothers*.

The amalgamation made good sense as both companies were competing for the same raw, both were involved in large-scale marketing of household products and both used similar distribution channels.

Margarine Unie was formed in 1927 when two rival margarine producers, Jurgens and Van den Bergh, joined forces. In the following years, other European companies, including *Calve delft*, *Hartog* and *Schicht* joined the *Margarine Unie*.

Lever Brothers was founded in 1885 by William Hesketh Lever, a wholesale grocer who used modern marketing methods to sell his *Sunlight* soap. Lever established soap factories around the world and in 1917 began to diversify into foods, acquiring fish, ice cream and canned foods businesses.

Between them, *Margarine Unie* and *Lever Brothers* had operations in over 40 countries. Their great entrepreneurial spirit and philanthropic approach to their employees and communities, in which they operated, remain at the heart of *Unilever's* business today.

These companies are now known as *Unilever* NV and *Unilever* PLC, the parent companies of the *Unilever Group*. The Group has grown to be one of the largest consumer goods businesses in the world through its commitment to the meeting everyday needs of people everywhere.

Unilever Baltic LLC was established in 1997 and operates in 3 Baltic countries: Estonia, Latvia and Lithuania, representing the fast moving consumer goods in 2 categories: Foods (*Lipton* tea, *Rama* and *Delma* margarine, *Knorr* soups, *Hellmann's* mayonnaise and ketchup) and Home & Personal Care (*OMO* detergent, *Cif* cleansing liquid, *Domestos* disinfecting liquid, *Timotei* shampoo, *Dove* soap and cream, *Rexona* deodorants).

Lattelekom

Lattelekom is the largest fixed telecommunications operator in Latvia. The company provides a large variety of services, from fixed telecommunications to data transmission, leased lines, Internet, etc. *Lattelekom* employs more than 4000 employees. By October 31, 2001, *Lattelekom* had 724 343 subscriber lines all over Latvia, 60% of which had been connected to the digital network.

Lattelekom was established on January 14, 1994. 51% of *Lattelekom* share capital belongs to the Republic of Latvia and 49% - to the international consortium *Tilts Communications*. 90% of *Tilts Communications* shares belongs to Finnish company *Sonera Holdings* B.V. and 10% - to the International Finance Corporation. Pursuant to the legislation of the Republic of Latvia *Lattelekom* has been granted exclusive rights to provide telecommunications services in Latvia. The said monopoly rights will expire on January 1, 2003.

YTD the company has invested more than 370 million Ls into the modernisation of the telecommunications network in Latvia.

In autumn, 2000 *Lattelekom Sakaru Sistēmas*, Lattelekom subsidiary, was established. *Lattelekom Sakaru Sistēmas* offers a whole variety of telecommunications equipment, from telephones to PABX.

Many of *Lattelekom* services are provided under a special brand name. *Verdi Informācijas sistēmas un konsultācijas* (*Verdi*) provides various IT services including e-business solutions, software applications, IT and system integration services and business consultations.

Lattelekom also provides Internet and directory inquiry services, which have been branded *Apollo* and *118* Directory Inquiries.

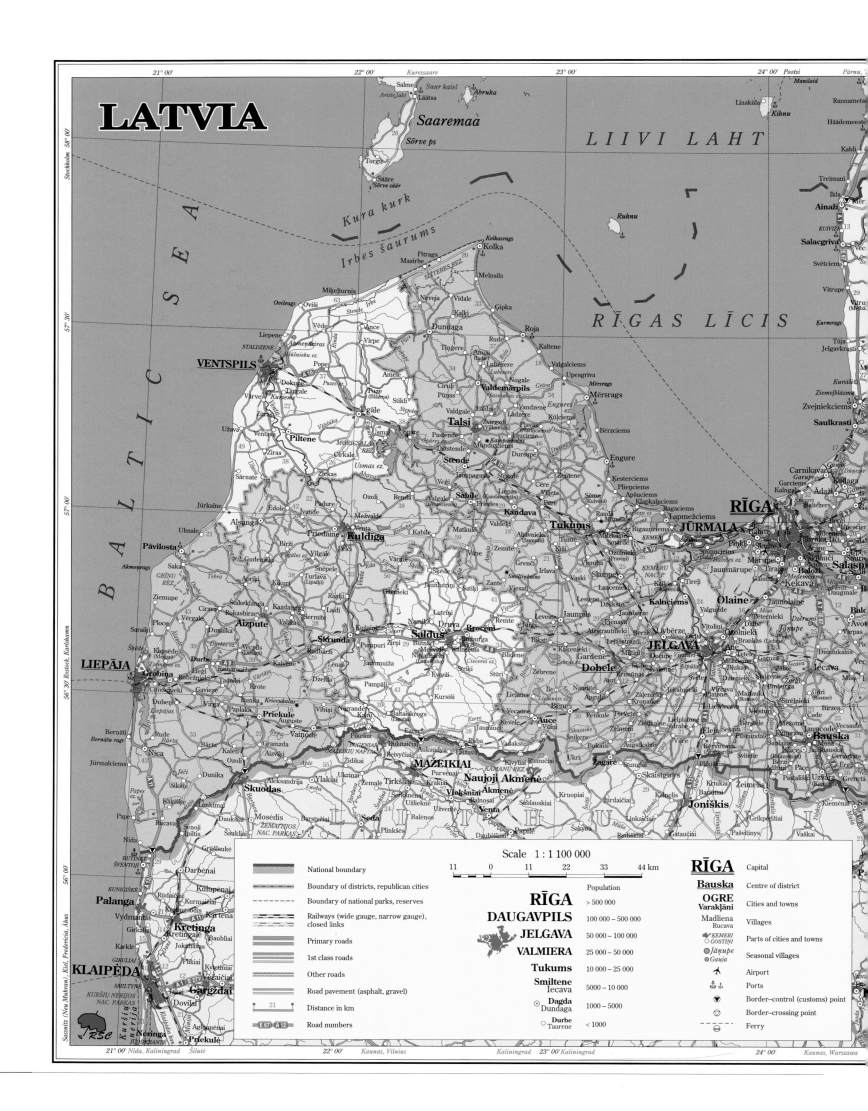

LATVIA

Scale 1 : 1 100 000

National boundary		
Boundary of districts, republican cities		
Boundary of national parks, reserves		
Railways (wide gauge, narrow gauge), closed links		
Primary roads		
1st class roads		
Other roads		
Road pavement (asphalt, gravel)		
21 Distance in km		
E 67 A 12 Road numbers		

Scale 1 : 1 100 000

11   0   11   22   33   44 km

Population

RĪGA	> 500 000
DAUGAVPILS	100 000 – 500 000
JELGAVA	50 000 – 100 000
VALMIERA	25 000 – 50 000
Tukums	10 000 – 25 000
Smiltene Iecava	5000 – 10 000
⊙ **Dagda** Dundaga	1000 – 5000
○ **Durbe** Taurene	< 1000

RĪGA	Capital
Bauska	Centre of district
OGRE **Varakļāni**	Cities and towns
Mādliena Rucava	Villages
✦ KEMERI ○ GOSTIŅI	Parts of cities and towns
⊙ Jāņupe ⊙ Gauja	Seasonal villages
✈	Airport
⚓ ⚓	Ports
▽	Border–control (customs) point
◌	Border–crossing point
⛴	Ferry

Table of distances in km

	AIZKRAUKLE	ALŪKSNE	BAUSKA	CĒSIS	DAUGAVPILS	DOBELE	GULBENE	JĒKABPILS	JELGAVA	KRĀSLAVA	KULDĪGA	LIEPĀJA	LIMBAŽI	LUDZA	MADONA	OGRE	PREIĻI	RĒZEKNE	RĪGA	SALDUS	TALSI	TUKUMS	VALKA	VALMIERA	VENTSPILS
AIZKRAUKLE	184	178	79	140	154	153	140	67	125	190	257	309	149	197	89	56	130	169	92	211	218	166	216	166	287
ALŪKSNE		46	267	121	218	279	44	149	242	215	358	418	155	131	95	204	181	124	199	327	319	267	103	112	388
BAUSKA			257	143	172	301	38	155	264	169	380	440	177	85	89	216	135	78	221	349	341	269	147	134	410
CĒSIS				157	233	75	219	146	62	269	180	228	158	276	168	75	209	248	61	133	168	116	126	237	
DAUGAVPILS					232	169	105	145	132	250	248	308	46	210	85	94	191	182	89	217	209	157	82	32	278
DOBELE						299	182	87	271	46	403	455	278	117	147	192	54	89	238	357	364	312	291	273	433
GULBENE							263	212	28	335	105	153	170	342	234	97	275	314	80	55	99	47	238	188	165
JĒKABPILS								111	226	179	342	402	139	123	51	178	145	88	183	311	303	251	109	96	372
JELGAVA									184	123	316	368	191	130	60	105	63	102	151	270	277	225	220	173	346
KRĀSLAVA										307	133	181	133	314	206	69	247	286	43	83	106	54	201	151	175
KULDĪGA											439	491	296	93	165	228	59	86	274	393	400	348	288	275	469
LIEPĀJA												309	498	390	253	431	470	219	101	146	170	377	327	123	
LIMBAŽI													89	249	446	338	201	379	418	159	53	59	93	317	267	60
LUDZA														256	131	93	237	228	90	218	210	158	96	46	279
MADONA															125	235	93	28	281	400	407	355	225	212	476
OGRE																127	106	97	173	292	299	247	160	113	368
PREIĻI																	168	207	36	155	162	110	93	113	231
RĒZEKNE																		253	372	379	327	197	184	448	
RĪGA																			128	120	68	158	108	189	
SALDUS																				87	72	286	236	113	
TALSI																					54	278	228	81	
TUKUMS																						236	176	123	
VALKA																							50	347	
VALMIERA																								297	
VENTSPILS																									

Latvian Coat-of-Arms

The Latvian coat-of-arms was created in 1920. On 29 November the competition ended, from which was selected the design submitted by graphic artist Vilhelms Krūmiņš. In the upper part of the shield on the coat-of-arms can be seen the sun motif. The lower part of the shield is divided into two areas: in the first is the image of a red lion on a silver background and in the second a silver griffin on a red background. The sun motif was often used as a coat-of-arms during the Latvian War of Independence, while the lion and the griffin are the coats-of-arms of the provinces that make up Latvia. The lion – Kurzeme and Zemgale, the griffin – Latgale and Vidzeme. Officially Latvia has three coats-of-arms – heraldic symbols: the State Greater Coat-of-Arms, the supplemented Lesser Coat-of-Arms and the State Lesser Coat-of-Arms. The Heraldic Commission determines the usage of the coat-of-arms in the Republic of Latvia.

The *Saeima* adopted the Law On the Coat-of-Arms of Latvia on 19 February 1998.

The Latvian Flag

The basis of the Latvian flag is the ancient war flag of *Cēsis* from the 12th century. The Rhyming Chronicle describes it in some 12 000 lines in German. In 1279, some 100 Latgalian soldiers arrived to assist the German Order of Teutonic Knights in *Cēsis*. The Latgalians had used a flag, which following ancient tradition was red with a white band.

In 1917, the 3rd Platoon of the 112th Company of the Latvian Riflemen Reserve Regiment used a red-white-red flag based on a design by Ansis Cīrulis. In May 1917 in Rīga, Jāzeps Grosvalds, Ansis Cīrulis, Kārlis Ubāns, and Voldemārs Tone designed a dark red flag with a narrow white band in the middle, and with a colour proportion of 2:1:2.

Under the red-white-red flag the 18 November 1918 Proclamation Act of the Republic of Latvia took place. The Latvian State flag was adopted in a law by the Constitutional Assembly and signed by the President Jānis Čakste on 15 June 1921. From 1940 to 1988, the red-white-red flag was banned, and for its use many Latvians were persecuted and repressed.

On 11 November 1988, the red-white-red flag was raised on the Holy Spirit tower of Rīga Castle, which was done by the former Latvian rifleman, actor Ēvalds Valters and the writer Alberts Bels.

On 16 January 1991, during the time of the barricades, the Supreme Council of the Republic of Latvia adopted amendments to laws, which approved the red-white-red flag as the national flag of the Republic of Latvia.

Kārlis Baumanis (1835-1905), Latvian composer, author of the Latvian National Anthem *Dievs, svētī Latviju!* (1873)

The song collection for men's choirs *Līgo* (1874) by Kārlis Baumanis

Latvian National Anthem

The Latvian national anthem was created during the national awakening period in the 19th century. Kārlis Baumanis, who was working at the time in St. Petersburg, sent to the Rīga Latvian Society on 26 March 1873, songs composed by him from his forthcoming collection *Līgo*. Among them was a 16 bar vocal miniature called *Dievs, svētī Latviju!* [God Bless Latvija] with the composer's own text. The song was not included in the programme of the Song Festival, however the conductor of the Baltic schoolteacher's seminar men's choir, Alberts Berndts, obtained a copy.

On 26 June 1873 in the Society House, the chairperson of the Rīga Latvian Society, Jānis Baumanis opened the First Latvian Song Festival. At the opening ceremony the Baltic schoolteacher's seminar men's choir sang *Dievs, svētī Latviju!*, which had not been included the officially approved songs of the festival programme, and was conducted by 19 year old student, later a choir conductor, Jānis Dreibergs. The song deeply moved the audience. The *Līgo* flag was carried in, the picture on which was also done on the basis of a design by Kārlis Baumanis.

In 1874, Kārlis Baumanis published his collection of songs for men's choirs *Līgo*, in which was included *Dievs, svētī Latviju!* The collection was banned and under the supervision of the Tsarist gendarmerie, in the Autumn of 1874, was burned on the banks of the *Daugava*. Only three copies of the book have survived to this day.

Dievs, svētī Latviju! was allowed to be included in the official programmes of song festivals only in 1895, in the programme of the 4th Latvian Song Festival. When the Republic of Latvia was proclaimed on 18 November 1918, the ceremony was begun and concluded with *Dievs, svētī Latviju!* by the Latvian Opera Choir conducted by Pauls Jozua. The status of official national anthem was granted on 7 June 1920 on the recommendation of Jāzeps Vītols.

In Latvia, when the anthem is played, it is expected that everyone stands, men will remove hats, but military personnel will salute. The anthem was banned during the Soviet occupation years. Many Latvians were persecuted and repressed for singing the anthem. It regained its status on 15 February 1990 in the Law On the Restoration of Latvian Historical Symbols.

The author of the words and music of the anthem, Kārlis Baumanis (1835-1905) was educated at the Valka Teachers Seminar, where under the influence of Jānis Cimze, he became interested in Latvian folk music and music theory. Baumanis worked as a teacher in St. Petersburg at the St. Anne's school, the Reformed school and the Smolnya Institute. In 1873, the Tsar Alexander II himself presented Baumanis with the Order of St. Anne and later he received the Order of St. Stanislav. In 1882, he returned to *Limbaži* in Latvia. Baumanis died in 1905 and is buried in the *Limbaži* cemetery.

Latvian National Epic

The epic *Lāčplēsis* [The Bearslayer] (1888) by the poet Andrejs Pumpurs is one of the outstanding achievements of Latvian literature. The epic heroically expresses a belief in the immortality of nations and the victory of freedom. In creating the epic *Lāčplēsis*, Pumpurs has utilised folktales and legends from Lielvarde and Lieljumprava, as well as the Chronicle of Henry Livonicus.